THE

SNEAKY

PARENT

THE
SNEAKY
PARENT

CRAFTY TACTICS FOR RAISING CHEERFUL, COOPERATIVE KIDS

By *New York Times* Best-Selling Authors
David Borgenicht and James Grace

QUIRK BOOKS
PHILADELPHIA

First edition published by Quirk Books in 2005 as *How to Con Your Kid*

Library of Congress Cataloging-in-Publication data available upon request.

ISBN: 978-1-68369-421-2

Printed in China

Typeset in Avenir, Gift Tag, Hello-Handmade Sans, and Sabon LT Std

Designed by Paige Graff based on a design by Michael Rogalski
Illustrations by Jason Schneider, www.jasonschneider.com
Production management by John J. McGurk

Quirk Books
215 Church Street
Philadelphia, PA 19106
quirkbooks.com

10 9 8 7 6 5 4 3 2 1

CONTENTS

Introduction   7

Grooming   **12**

Get Your Kid to Let You Brush Their Hair   14

Get Your Kid to Brush Their Teeth   18

Get Your Kid to Wash Up   22

Get Your Kid a Haircut   25

Get Your Kid to Take Medicine   30

Getting Ready   **34**

Get Your Kid Dressed   36

Get Your Kid to Keep Their Clothes On   40

Get Your Kid Moving   44

Get Your Kid to the Doctor or Dentist   48

Get Your Kid to School   53

Get Your Kid to Put On Sunscreen   57

Good Behavior   **62**

Get Your Kid to Meet Someone New   64

Get Your Kid to Write a Thank-You Note   68

Get Your Kid to Let You Leave   71

Get Your Kid to Sleep Over with Family or Friends   76

Get Your Kid to Sit Still   80

Get Your Kid to Survive an Airplane Trip   83

Get Your Kid to Talk Quietly   87

Get Your Kid to Stop Crying   90

Get Your Kid to Stop Whining   95

Get Your Kid to Stop Throwing a Tantrum   98

Get Your Kid to Put Something Down   101

Around the House   **106**

Get Your Kid to Share   108

Get Your Kids to Stop Annoying Each Other   112

Get Your Kid to Help with Chores   116

Get Your Kid to Clean Up   123

Get Your Kid to Limit Screen Time   128

Get Your Kid to Play Alone   131

Mealtime and Bedtime   **136**

Get Your Kid to Eat   138

Get Your Kid to Go Out to Dinner   144

Get Your Kid to Take a Bath   149

Get Your Kid to Wash Their Hair   153

Get Your Kid to Go to Bed   157

Get Your Kid to Go to Sleep   162

Appendix   **166**

About the Authors   **173**

Acknowledgments   **174**

INTRODUCTION

This is the book your kids don't want you to read.

This is the book that will give you the skills, the know-how, and the street smarts to beat your children at the only game they're better at than you are—being children. Sure, they're smaller than you and, theoretically, not as smart as you. And, sure, you are the grown-up, so whatever you say goes, no matter what, right?

But in the real world, and especially with today's mode of parenting (in which many of us attempt to talk to our kids as if they're adults—our first mistake), that's not how it works. That's just not how kids play the game.

For children, especially those between the ages of 2 and 7, every day is a struggle between wanting to be more in control of their own lives and wanting to still be your little baby. As infants, all they had to do was cry and you'd come running. Why shouldn't that same approach work now, especially if they can add whining, cajoling, and negotiating to the mix? Just because they have the capacity for empathy and reason doesn't mean they think it'll get them what they want any faster!

Why shouldn't they spend all day completely naked? Why can't they have ice cream as an after-school snack? Kids don't know you're supposed to get dressed before you go anywhere or that candy isn't the base of the food pyramid. Kids don't know they aren't allowed to play on your phone 24/7 just like you do. Kids don't know there isn't an unlimited supply of money in your wallet for buying toys whenever they want or that tantrums aren't the primary negotiating tool of all great litigators. (Come to think of it, some great litigators don't know that, either.) Kids don't realize that getting a haircut isn't an ancient form of torture, that nail trimming doesn't hurt, or that there's such a thing as an inside voice.

That's where you come in. You have to educate them somehow—or otherwise convince them to do what you want. That can be accomplished in a variety of ways.

Sometimes it's enough to lay the groundwork—give them the benefit of the doubt, treat them like responsible and intelligent individuals, teach them why things are the way they are.

But other times, you'll need to be a bit, well, craftier. You'll need to trick, distract, or redirect your child so that they fall in line. This book gives you the essential tools and knowledge to do just that.

This book contains all the information you need to pull a fast one on your kid—to convince them to behave exactly the way you want them to, anytime, anywhere. You'll learn classic techniques, like being "A Little Sneaky" (offering choices that make your child feel as though they're in control, when in reality you're the one setting the terms), getting "Pretty Sneaky" with more complicated ruses, and turning dreaded activities into fun and games. You'll master the art of misdirection and gain time-honored parenting skills you can use to get your kids to bend to your will—without them ever realizing it.

To come up with the suggestions that follow, we not only tapped into the vast arsenal of parental weapons we have used on our own children—David has two kids, Sophie and Max; James has three, Avery, Cooper, and Dustin—we also surveyed dozens of other parents and experts (doctors, family therapists) in order to provide you with a comprehensive guide to the simplest ploys and best misdirection methods available. All are parent tested and approved, and we offer several options so that you can choose the trick that best suits the situation, the need, and your particular child. What's more, you'll learn the basic principles to invent sneaky moves of your very own.

We hope you'll use this book wisely—and that you'll keep it in a safe place. After all, kids are learning to read earlier and earlier these days, and you don't want it to fall into the wrong hands. Feel free to share it with other parents once your own children have finally gained the capacity to reason (or at least when they're on to you and your schemes).

And remember: We are the parents. We are bigger, smarter, and craftier. We don't have to let them push us around—and in fact, nobody has to push at all! With just a little sneaky plotting, you can keep kids happy, healthy, and well-behaved without fighting. It might even be fun!

—David and James

GET YOUR KID TO LET YOU BRUSH THEIR HAIR

Isn't there an old wives' tale advising one hundred strokes before bed? Yeah, right. Most parents would happily settle for ten strokes before school. The "bed head" look may be popular with teenagers, but does it work on a three-year-old?

LAYING THE GROUNDWORK

- K.I.S.S.—Keep It Short, Stupid. If your child really has a hard time getting their hair brushed, keep it short. It's simpler.

- Wash their hair every other night, using both a kids' shampoo and a separate kids' conditioner. (To minimize annoyance with the process, put the shampoo on first, then the conditioner, and rinse only once.) This should make it less unruly.

- If your child has curly hair, wash it only two or three times a week. Apply conditioner (no shampoo) or a no-suds shampoo.

- Use a "no tangle" spray to reduce the formation of knots.

- Seek expert advice. Ask your hairdresser which type of hairbrush will work best for your child's hair type to minimize pain.

PRETTY SNEAKY

- Comb or brush their hair while they are in the shower or bath—don't wait for a larger battle later.

- Start at the bottom (where the knots are) and work your way up. This will minimize discomfort. Hold the hair above the knots so that you don't pull at your child's scalp.

- For kids who enjoy having special ribbons and barrettes in their hair, make these accessories an incentive. Tell your kid that you're going to make them look like a princess, a favorite character, or a friend who always wears barrettes.

- Brush your child's hair while they're in front of the television or computer, or better yet, while your spouse reads aloud to them. When distracted, kids are less likely to complain.

A LITTLE SNEAKY

"Do you want to watch a TV show or a video while I brush your hair?"

"Do you want me to brush your hair when it's dry or wet it first with a spray bottle?"

"Do you want to brush your hair or should I?"

BRUSH LITTLE BABY

To the tune of "Hush Little Baby."

Brush little baby, don't move about
I'm gonna get those knots right out

If those knots won't come undone
We're gonna brush to the count of one

If the count of one won't do
We're gonna brush to the count of two

If the number two's too wee
We're gonna brush to the count of three

If after three you still need more
We're gonna brush to the count of four

If the knots are still alive
We're gonna brush to the count of five

If your hair still needs a fix
We're gonna brush to the count of six

And so on . . .

GAMES PARENTS PLAY

The Search for Witch Knotty

Pretend to be on the hunt for a grumpy witch named "Knotty" who lives somewhere in your child's hair. Find her, "chase" her out (brushing your child's hair to do this), and then tell your child that she's escaped—to the next strands that need brushing. Your child laughs, and the hair gets brushed. (This trick works with any other creature hunt—try searching out mice, rabbits, and so on.)

IF THEY'RE ON TO YOU

Let your child comb their own hair. Explain to everyone how independent your child is and hope for the best. The old adage holds: They won't go off to college with unbrushed hair. Or maybe they will, but in that case it will be a fashion statement.

GET YOUR KID TO BRUSH THEIR TEETH

Children should brush their teeth as often as we do—twice a day. This is, of course, easier said than done. Until the age of five, they don't really have the coordination (or patience) to do it on their own. (Mostly, they don't have the patience.) But it must be done—after all, a two-year-old with halitosis and tooth decay is not a pleasant thing to behold.

LAYING THE GROUNDWORK

- Getting kids fired up about brushing their teeth is all about the prep. Begin when they are infants by massaging their gums. Hype it up when you brush your own teeth. Let your toddler put your toothpaste on your toothbrush. "Ooh" and "aah" over how great it feels to have that fresh, minty feeling.

- If your dentist is good with children (an important criterion), bring your child along. (If you will be writhing in pain or very nervous, get a sitter.)

- Allow your child to pick the toothbrush and toothpaste. As always, the lure of child-focused marketing can sometimes work to your advantage—there are plenty of licensed character toothbrushes to choose from, and lots of candy-tasting toothpaste flavors.

PRETTY SNEAKY

- Be the dentist's chair. Have your child lie on your reclined body—their back to your chest. Pretend to be the dentist examining their beautiful teeth. Brush their teeth while you're there.

- Ask your child to show their favorite toy how to brush. Have the toy give encouragement. For example, Cookie Monster might say, "Me want to brush teeth but me not know how! Who will show Cookie?" Brush your child's teeth as a demonstration for the toy and then allow your child to brush the toy's teeth afterward.

- Pretend the toothbrush is electric, even if it's not. Turn it "on," making a buzzing noise as you brush.

- Don't call it "brushing teeth," say that you are "painting teeth." Ask your child what color they want their teeth to be, then pretend to paint them as you brush.

- Turn the toothbrush into a character itself—"Toothy," "Tooth Bader Ginsburg," or "Bristley Spears," perhaps. Talk in a funny voice, and tell your child that "Toothy" really wants to explore the inside of their mouth. It seems silly, but it can work.

- Don't call it "toothpaste," call it "magic wishing paste." Your child gets to make a wish when done brushing.

A LITTLE SNEAKY

"Do you want me to brush your teeth, or do you want to brush your teeth yourself and then I will brush them?"

"Do you want to race? The winner is the one who brushes the longest."

"Do you want me to start with the top teeth or the bottom teeth?"

BRUSH BACK PADDYWHACK

To the tune of "This Old Man."

Brush on top
Brush below
Brush your teeth
1, 2, 3—Go!

With a brush back paddywhack
Brusha brush your teeth
Brush on top and underneath
Brush 'em fast
Brush 'em slow
It's so healthy
Don't you know?

With a brush back paddywhack
Brusha brush your teeth
Brush on top and underneath
Brush a smile

Brush a frown
Right side up
Or upside down

With a brush back paddywhack
Brusha brush your teeth
Brush on top and underneath

Find the Mouse

Tell your child that you need to find "the tooth mouse" (or runaway zoo
animal, missing princess, shy dragon, or whatever else will capture your child's
imagination). Use the toothbrush as a tool for "searching" your child's mouth—
giving names to the spaces, such as caves, nooks, or castle rooms. Continue the
narrative as long as it takes to get those teeth clean.

Call in the experts. Ask for a special phone call or a face-to-face meeting in
which your child's dentist explains the importance of toothbrushing and the
sufficiently "yucky" consequences of neglecting the task. Use visuals.

GET YOUR KID TO WASH UP

Five out of five doctors agree that frequent washing is the key to preventing colds, flu, and other viruses from infecting your child (and your home). It's also the only sure way to prevent finger paints and chocolate ice cream from ending up on the furniture.

LAYING THE GROUNDWORK

- Make hand washing a habit. Kids who wash their hands multiple times every day will feel uncomfortable if they forget and will seek to do it themselves. For some children, instilling this habit can take months; for others, only weeks. It's worth the effort in the long run.

- Be a role model. If you duck out of the bathroom unwashed, your child will notice and feel they can do the same.

- Let your child wash their own hands as much as possible. You do "the final wipe."

- Purchase a special stepstool that is your child's own. Let them carry it over to the sink—and make a big deal about how proud you are that they are washing up.

- Keep portable wipes or hand sanitizer with you when not at home.

- Let your child pick out the soap and a special washrag.

- Turn the washing-up experience into a play activity. Cups and bowls, turkey basters, even bath toys can make the washing-up process more fun.

- Get a washable marker and draw a funny face or picture on your child's hands so that they have something to wash off. "Wash Away the Monster" always works.

- Play a favorite song, and tell your child that you wonder if they're "fast enough to wash up by the time the song is over."

- Purchase a washrag that looks like an animal (usually a duck or a fish) and turn the "washing up" into a puppet show: Who, after all, could refuse to be washed by "Quacky the Duck"?

A LITTLE SNEAKY

"Do you want to wash your hands at the sink, or should I bring a washrag over?"

"Do you want the liquid soap or the bar soap?"

"Do you want to wash with warm or cold water?"

THIS IS THE WAY WE WASH OUR HANDS

To the tune of "Here We Go 'Round the Mulberry Bush."

This is the way we roll up our sleeves
Roll up our sleeves, roll up our sleeves
This is the way we roll up our sleeves
After we go to the potty [BEFORE WE EAT OUR DINNER]

Repeat with each part of the process:

This is the way we put on the soap . . .

This is the way we scrub our hands . . .

This is the way we rinse our hands . . .

This is the way we dry our hands . . .

IF THEY'RE ON TO YOU

Teach germ theory. Cover the basics—how everything they touch outside has germs on it, and might make them sick. Make them understand how truly "yucky" unclean hands can be.

THE CHALLENGE:

GET YOUR KID A HAIRCUT

Most children are afraid of haircuts because they think the process will hurt—and who can blame them? You see a stranger coming at your head with a pair of scissors, and you might be afraid, too. Plus, haircuts require sitting completely still for anywhere from ten to thirty minutes. How do you get your little rock star to agree to a visit with Vidal Sassoon?

LAYING THE GROUNDWORK

- Tell your child when you're going to get your hair cut, as a way to subtly teach them that it's something grown-ups *and* kids do. Better yet—let them come along with you to see how it all works and that it won't hurt.

- Find a good kid-friendly barber with lots of toys, games, and other entertaining items.

- Don't say you're going to the barber—learn the barber's name and say you're going to your friend's place, calling the barber by name.

- Do it yourself—set up a "barber shop" or "salon" in your kitchen. Invite your child in for their appointment. Ask them to bring play money with which to pay (and to tip) you or let them use real coins. Play fun, kid-friendly music—let your child pick. Allow them to wet their own hair with a spray bottle (don't scold if they get you wet). Talk throughout the haircut. Tell jokes. Ask questions. Start slow—do not give your child an aggressive haircut. Begin with a trim. After the haircut, comment repeatedly on what a "big kid" they were. Tell your friends. Tell your neighbors. Celebrate the milestone in some way.

- Enlist a second adult or older sibling. Use previously mentioned tactics but add an element of immobilization. Your child can sit on the adult's or sibling's lap or in a highchair during the haircut. Have the second adult distract them.

- Use a video or a snack or both. (Caution: The snack may get hairy.) Work very quickly. Let go of the idea that it all needs to happen in one sitting. A haircut may happen over the course of a week.

HAIRCUTS ARE FUN

To the tune of "Here Comes the Sun."

Haircuts are fun
Little darlin'
Haircuts are fun

And I say
It's all right

Little darlin'
Your hair's so long I cannot see you
Little darlin'
It seems like months since it's been cut

Haircuts are fun
Little darlin'
Haircuts are fun
And I say
It's all right

Little darlin'
You know that haircuts will not harm you
Little darlin'
You know that I'll be by your side

Haircuts are fun
Little darlin'
Haircuts are fun
And I say
It's all right

Hair, hair, haircuts are fun
Hair, hair, haircuts are fun

"Do you want to sit or stand when you get your haircut?"

"Do you want me to read to you or tell you a story?"

"Do you want [BARBER'S NAME] to spray your hair or rinse it?"

Barber Shop

Two weeks prior to the date of the impending haircut, begin the process of desensitization. Introduce the idea of their doll getting a new haircut. Use subtle phrasing such as "Wouldn't Barbie look great with a new hairdo?" or "Aren't Elmo's bangs getting long?" Design a small barber chair out of building blocks or popsicle sticks. Place the doll in the chair. Show the child how to wet the doll's hair. Provide pretend scissors for the cut. Supply money to be given to the child by the thankful doll. Gush about how fabulous the doll looks. Schedule the doll's next appointment. Bring up the haircut over dinner, at bedtime, or while driving the car. Remind the child of how well it went.

As the event nears, up the proverbial ante. Set up a role play about a person getting a haircut, but don't tell your child that *their* hair will eventually be cut. Begin to break down their fears and anxieties before they even know they have them: Take your child through each of the steps of a real haircut. Give your child a water bottle, and let them wet your hair. Sit on a chair and let your child "cut" your hair with their fingers. (Do not give your child actual scissors. The trick won't work if your child looks at the results and is afraid.) Smile a lot. Give your child "money" as payment and an additional "tip." Have the "money" be good for the purchase of something fun.

IF THEY'RE ON TO YOU

- When all else fails, let your kid wear their hair long. When it starts to annoy them, they'll probably change their tune, but if it doesn't, what's the big deal?

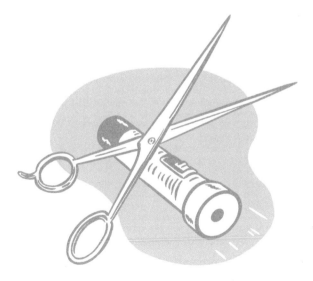

GET YOUR KID TO TAKE MEDICINE

Just a spoonful of sugar makes the medicine go down, a wise woman (Mary Poppins, the original Super Nanny) once said. Depending on your child and depending on the medicine, it may take more than a spoonful of sugar.

LAYING THE GROUNDWORK

- Begin by educating your child, even when they are very young. Explain what medication is and how it helps them get healthy. Be clear that taking the medicine is nonnegotiable, and that "we all do it."

- Give them as much of a choice as you can about the process—who gives the medicine to them, when to take it (within reason), and what drinks they can choose from afterward.

- If using a medicine syringe to squirt the liquid into their mouth (not for subcutaneous injection), aim for the back of the cheek. Harder to spit out, easier to slide down.

- Let them give you your medicine whenever you have to take it—this will show them that medicine is not so bad after all. Thank them profusely for helping with such an important chore.

PRETTY SNEAKY

- Cold temperatures mask unpleasant flavors, so keep the medicine chilled. If that isn't enough to mask the taste, mixing cold medicine into equally cold foods—pudding, applesauce, yogurt, or ice slush—may work. To make an easy slush, break off a piece of a popsicle, and microwave it briefly until slushy. Offer the rest of the popsicle as a reward after your child takes the medicine.

- Mix the medicine with soda. Orange or grape soda, served very cold, will disguise the taste of just about any liquid medicine—and is a treat for your child. Adjust the mixture to the nastiness of the medicine.

- Play Mary Poppins—administer the medicine with one spoon and follow promptly with a spoonful of chocolate syrup (load both spoons in advance). Among its many other beneficial properties, chocolate really eliminates the aftertaste of just about any medicine.

- Let your child decide where to take the medicine—yielding one small element of control to your kid often does the trick.

A LITTLE SNEAKY

"Do you want to take your medicine in the bathroom or in your bedroom?"
"Do you want to use a little cup or a syringe?"
"Do you want to take your medicine quickly or slowly?"

THE DRINKER'S CHEER

Teach the following cheer to your child—they should know what to do at the end.

Gimme a "D"
Gimme an "R"
Gimme an "I"
Gimme an "N"
Gimme a "K"
What does that spell?
DRINK!

I can't hear you!
DRINK!
What are we gonna do with the medicine?
DRINK!
(they drink)
Hip Hip Hooray!

Superhero Juice

Give the medicine a special name, like "Pink Super Juice" or something equally silly but catchy. Explain that your child gets more superpowers with every dose. Fashion them a cape out of an old apron. Give the medicine, and watch their powers grow. Be creative—include various faux feats of strength.

For truly recalcitrant types, it takes two adults to manage the following last-resort approach. Lay your child on their back. One adult pinches the nostrils shut (which forces them to open their mouth to breathe) while holding their head steady. If your child doesn't open their mouth, a little pressure at the temporomandibular joint (the jawbone joints near the child's ears) will force open the mouth. The second adult then administers liquid medicine, preferably via a squirt from a syringe, and then shuts the child's mouth. Watch for the swallow, which will occur quickly because your child wants to breathe, and then allow the nostrils to open while keeping your child flat and still to prevent choking.

Be aware that this technique will really make a child angry and/or upset and there are no guarantees that the medicine will stay down. But your child will be far more likely to be compliant for the next dose. It might sound horrible, and we want to emphasize that this is for truly necessary medication only, and only when all other methods have failed. But our pediatrician learned this method from the nurses at a children's hospital emergency department.

GETTING READY

THE CHALLENGE:

GET YOUR KID DRESSED

Maybe it's that kids prefer to be in control; maybe it's that they don't like things being pulled over their heads—either way, getting dressed can be a daily struggle if not handled correctly.

- Make it a policy to get your child dressed first thing—before you even leave their room in the morning.
- Let your child pick the clothes for the day—with guidance, of course. This will invest them in the process.
- Buy shirts that are easy to put on—tops that button up or have wide collars. These will help you avoid having to pull a tight shirt over their head.
- Make sure the clothes fit your kid. Clothing that is too small is never comfortable.

- Turn getting dressed into a race: "Let's see if we can get you dressed before I count to twenty."

- Use the carrot-and-stick method of persuasion: "We have to get dressed if we're going to make it to the [ZOO/MUSEUM/TOY STORE]."
- Teach your child how to get dressed by themselves (as much as possible). Tape pictures of clothing on their dresser drawers so that they know where everything is located.

"Do you want to wear this outfit or that outfit?"

"Do you want to put on your pants first, or your shirt?"

"Do you want to get dressed standing up or lying down?"

THE CLOTHES-Y POKEY
To the tune of "The Hokey Pokey."

You put your right arm in
You put your right arm out
You put your right arm in (*place your child's arm through the sleeve of the shirt*)
And you shake it all about
You do the Clothes-y Pokey and you turn yourself around
That's what it's all about

Repeat with other body parts until they're fully dressed:
You put your left arm in . . . (*left sleeve*)

You put your right leg in . . . (*right pant leg*)
You put your left leg in . . . (*left pant leg*)
You put your right foot in . . . (*right sock and shoe*)
You put your left foot in . . . (*left sock and shoe*)
You put your whole self in . . . (*jacket*)

The Clothing Store

This popular game turns getting dressed into a role-playing activity that's fun for everyone. Needless to say, you are the salesperson and your child is the customer. Feel free to embellish or change the terminology as needed.

You: Good morning. Are you looking for something to wear?

Child: Yes!

You: Well, you've come to the right place. Let me show you what we've got. (*Take out two shirts.*) We have two lovely shirts on sale today—which one do you like? (*Your child picks one.*) Excellent choice—let's see if it fits. (*Put it on your child, and take them to the mirror to look.*) Now, what else can I interest you in—pants, perhaps?

Child: Yes!

You: All righty—let's see. Do you like these or these? (*Hold up two pairs. Your child picks one.*) Lovely. Let's try them on. (*Put the pants on your child, and take them to the mirror to look.*)

Continue the game until they're fully clothed. And don't forget to make them pay at the end!

IF THEY'RE ON TO YOU

Establish a morning routine and stick to it. Start when your child is very young, and decide when getting dressed fits in—first thing, after breakfast, whatever works. Eventually, your kid will understand that getting dressed is just a part of getting the day started, and will fight you much less fervently.

GET YOUR KID TO KEEP THEIR CLOTHES ON

You know how a dog will attempt to chew off a bandage as soon as you put one on its paw? This is why dogs wear those plastic cones post-op. It isn't practical (or even legal) to restrain your child in such a manner to keep them from removing key articles of clothing—but the motivation is the same. Kids, like dogs, hate the feeling of being restricted in their movement.

LAYING THE GROUNDWORK

- If you're dealing with an inveterate nudist, buy articles of clothing that are difficult to remove—zippers and Velcro may be easy to get on, but they're also easy to take off. Go with lace-up shoes (and double knot them) and button-up coats and shirts. Purchase "onesies" that button under the crotch.

- Teach your child how to put on their own clothing, and then praise, praise, praise them. Telling them how proud you are and "what a big kid" they are goes a long way as an incentive.

- Tell them they have to wear their [HAT/COAT/GLOVES] when you reach your ultimate destination, but that they can take them off in the car before you get there. This allows your child to agree to your demands with dignity and a feeling of independence.

PRETTY SNEAKY

- Draw or sew faces onto the sleeves of coats, the palms of mittens, and the tops of hats. Familiar characters are best—kids will always agree to putting on a coat if it's not just an article of clothing but, rather, a friend.

- Similarly, animal-themed hats, coats, and gloves will work more effectively than standard attire.

- A warm, plush Halloween costume can provide an emergency alternative to an unpopular parka. They'll be more inclined to stay in their lion suit or cat hat.

- For hat haters, try earmuffs. They're less restrictive (and less warm), but at least they keep the ears cozy. And they come in duck, bear, and penguin forms.

A LITTLE SNEAKY

"Do you want to wear that coat or this coat?"

"Do you want to wear your gloves or your mittens?"

"Do you want to put on your coat first, or your hat?"

PUTTIN' ON YOUR COAT

To the tune of "Puttin' On the Ritz."

Oh when it's cold
And you want to go
Outside to play
And run or jump just like a goat
Just put on your coat

And when your hands
Are too cold to stand
Outside your pants
And you just need some warmth and love
Just put on your gloves.

Though you may think nudity is funny
Wouldn't you rather be warm just like a bunny?
When it's sunny.

So if your mom
And dad just say
"There's no way
You're going out of here like that"
Just put on your hat.

IF THEY'RE ON TO YOU

When in doubt, layer—at least three layers in the winter. That way, when the coat comes off, at least there are two layers left. Use thermals or long underwear for the bottom layer.

GET YOUR KID MOVING

Sometimes they're simply enjoying themselves too much to consider leaving (running in circles with a pot on your head is *so* much fun); other times it's that they're just too tired to take one more step (this is when your kid turns boneless and floppy). Whatever the case, it's almost always a struggle to get kids moving, whether you're trying to get them out the door or down the block.

LAYING THE GROUNDWORK

- Give your child a reasonable amount of forewarning if you know you're going to be headed somewhere—at least an hour or two in advance—to get them ready mentally. Remind them a few minutes before you want to get ready to go.

- Have your child pick something to take with you on your outing—this will invest them in the trip.

- "Talk up" whatever it is you're headed to: "I wonder if we'll see any rainbows on the way to Grandma's." (The negative version also works: "I hope they don't run out of ice cream before we get there—we're taking soooooooo long.")

- Put your child in charge of making sure that their doll or toy is ready to go on time.

- The old "I'll race you to the corner" trick can be used in a variety of circumstances—but it's particularly useful in this one. Tell your child to say, "Ready, set—GO!" and take off. Let them win. Challenge them again, until you reach your destination.

- An alternate version of racing is, "Do you think you can make it to the corner by the time I finish singing the ABC song?"

- Take note of landmarks or points of interest in the direction you are headed, and then point them out enthusiastically to encourage forward momentum. "Hey look! A horse sculpture! A duck! A cool plant! Let's go see it!" Or "Hey! We're about to pass the giant doughnut on the side of the road up ahead! Can you see it yet?"

- Play "Follow the Leader" or "Marching Band," taking turns making forward progress. Don't forget to say "Oompah, oompah" as you march.

A LITTLE SNEAKY

"Do you want to walk fast or just run?"

"Should we walk or take the stroller?"

"Do you want to walk side by side or single file?"

WE'RE GOING TO THE GROCERY STORE
To the tune of "Michael, Row Your Boat Ashore."

We're going to the grocery store
Hallelujah
We're going to the grocery store
Hallelujah

Replace "grocery store" with other destinations as appropriate.

GAMES PARENTS PLAY

Turn your leisurely stroll into a game of tag. Say, "You can't catch me!" or "Not it!" and run up ahead, taking care not to get so far ahead that your child is left unattended. Your child will set chase, and you'll be on your way. Once they catch you, you chase them, and so on . . .

IF THEY'RE ON TO YOU

- Remember that the process of getting your kids out the door always takes at least twice as long as it should. So if you're accustomed to allowing fifteen minutes for prep, double your allotted time and leave thirty.

- Get comfortable with the good old "pick them up and run" technique. If you do it with a smile on your face and carry them in a funny way (flying like an airplane, upside down, or like a sack of potatoes), they may even laugh despite the fact that you're essentially dragging them away against their will.

GET YOUR KID TO THE DOCTOR OR DENTIST

Getting children to feel comfortable about going to the doctor or dentist is tough, even without the negative propaganda they encounter in cartoons and movies. Virtually every visit to the doctor in the early months means receiving a shot, being poked and prodded, or just hanging out with a bunch of sick kids. Dentists come at them with strange-looking instruments, force them to open their mouths against their will, and sit them in a frightening-looking chair. But with a little pregame prep, and a few sneaky strategies, what seems like a necessary evil can actually become a fun outing.

LAYING THE GROUNDWORK

- Let your child know when *you* have an appointment with the doctor or dentist—this will help them learn that it's something everyone does. Take them with you if you can so that they can see what goes on, and so that they aren't afraid.

- Try to find a doctor and a dentist who really know how to deal with children—one positive sign is if they have "fun" offices, with lots of books, toys, and games in the waiting room (and maybe even toys for kids to hang on to for comfort during the appointment). You can ask doctors or dentists directly how they handle anxious kids.

- Don't refer to your doctor as "the doctor"—make them seem more like a friend you see occasionally. When your child has an appointment, don't say that "we have an appointment with Doctor Jacobs"—say, enthusiastically, "We're going to see our friend Doctor Jacobs today!"

- Schedule appointments as early in the day as possible. This will give you more time to do something fun afterward, and you're more likely to be seen on time, reducing the wait.

PRETTY SNEAKY

- Play doctor or dentist at home, with each other as well as with dolls and stuffed animals. Give your child a "checkup" with a toy stethoscope and a tooth exam with a mirror and toothbrush—then let them do the same for you.

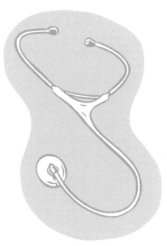

- Prepare your children for shots and medicine by giving them to the dolls and stuffed animals first. If a shot is coming their way, explain that shots don't actually hurt any more than a small pinch.

- If you have time (and your child isn't ill, of course), plan a special outing for after the doctor's or dentist's appointment. Use this as the carrot—"Guess where we're going today after the doctor? The Children's Museum!"

A LITTLE SNEAKY

"Do you want a popsicle or an ice cream cone after the dentist today?"

"Which [BOOK/TOY/DOLL] are you going to take to the dentist today?"

"Are you going to ask for a sticker or a toy from Doctor _____?"

"Let's count your teeth so that you can tell Doctor _____ how many you've got now."

I FEEL GREAT

To the tune of "I Feel Good," by James Brown. Sing this song when getting ready to head off for your appointment or in the doctor's waiting room.

I feel great
Doodle-oodle-oodle-oo
I hope the doctor's [DENTIST'S] not late
Doodle-oodle-oodle-oo

I feel great
Doodle-oodle-oodle-oo
I hope we don't have to wait
Doodle-oodle-oodle-oo

So great!
So great!
It must be something I ate.
Doo Doo Doo Doo Doo Doo!

Variation:
I feel sick
Doodle-oodle-oodle-oo
I hope I get better quick
Doodle-oodle-oodle-oo

I feel sick
Doodle-oodle-oodle-oo
The doctor [DENTIST] knows a few tricks
Doodle-oodle-oodle-oo

So sick!
So sick!
I need help quick.
Doo Doo Doo Doo Doo Doo!

I Went to the Doctor (or Dentist)

Similar to the classic road game "I Went on a Trip," "I Went to the Doctor (or Dentist)" is a great game to play in the waiting room or on the way to the appointment. It lets you talk about the subject without making it seem frightening.

1. Tell your child to say, "We went to the doctor and we saw a _____," and have them name something at the doctor's office.

2. Then you say, "We went to the doctor's office and we saw a _____ and a _____," naming the item your child named and adding one of yours.

3. Your child now says, "We went to the doctor and we saw a _____ and a _____ and a _____," naming their first item, your item, and adding one of their own.

4. Continue the game until you get bored or the doctor is able to see you.

IF THEY'RE ON TO YOU

If your child is visibly nervous about visiting the doctor or dentist, don't dismiss their feelings—acknowledge their concerns, then redirect the conversation to the fun parts of seeing the doctor. "I know you're nervous about going to the doctor, but it's going to be fine. Besides, he's going to look in your ears to see if he can find any kitty cats, and he'll bop your knee with his bopping tool!"

GET YOUR KID TO SCHOOL

Some kids wake up excited for school every day. If you didn't get one of these kids, you'll need to overcome their natural reluctance. You'll need to work on talking up the day, offering them no better alternative, and making school fun.

LAYING THE GROUNDWORK

- From the moment your child awakens, start talking about school—in a casual manner. Don't overdramatize the situation or sound apologetic about it. Just talk as if you assume that it's a part of the day.

- Involve them in getting ready. When picking clothes, say, "What would you like to wear to school today?" Ask them to help make lunch, or decide what shoes or coat to wear.

- Pick a special item or toy for your child to take to school and show to the other students or the teachers.

- Have a special "pre-school" and "post-school" routine. Play a special "going to school" song just before you leave the house or in the car on the way to school. Play in the park together after school—or make a regular trip to the ice cream or smoothie store.

- Learn the names of the children at school, especially the ones your child regularly plays with. Work them into your pre-school spin.

PRETTY SNEAKY

- Find out the weekly schedule so you can "talk up" whatever it is they're going to do that day. Tell your child, "It's a very special day today at school—it's [ART/MUSIC/COOKING/STORY] day!" As long as you use an emphatic tone of voice, they'll get excited.

- Tell your child that it's a special "wishing" day for every kid who goes to school that day—and that when you pick them up, he'll get to make a wish for anything they want.

- Take your child shopping for "school stuff"—a lunchbox, backpack, new coat, etc. Let them pick items they really love, but tell them that they can only use them for school. A Bluey lunchbox or Spider-Man backpack is a powerful motivator.

- With your child's help, make a special "school map" that shows the route you'll take to school every day. Keep it in a special place, and when it's almost time to leave for school, tell your child that "you can't forget your map" and that you need their help remembering how to get to school.

"Do you want to take pasta or a sandwich to school today?"
"Do you want to go the regular way or the secret way to school today?"
"Do you want to wear your red sweater or your blue sweater to school today?"

TODAY'S A SCHOOL DAY

To the tune of "Frere Jacques."

Today is Monday
Today is Monday
All day long
All day long
Monday is a school day
Monday is a school day
All day long
All day long

Repeat on other days of the week, substituting the correct day.

GAMES PARENTS PLAY

Make That Sound

Tell your child that you're going to play "Make That Sound" on the way to school. The game can be played in the car or while walking.

1. Decide how many sounds your child will have to make on the way to school. (Approximately one sound per minute of travel time should do the trick.)

2. Start the game by saying, "I hear a sound that a _____ makes—make that sound!"

3. While your child thinks, hum a bit of "thinking music." If you don't know the tune from *Jeopardy!*, try the ABC song.

4. Repeat as necessary.

5. Keep score, and praise them extensively to keep things moving along.

IF THEY'RE ON TO YOU

- If your child is overly resistant to going to school, it could be an indication that they are bored, afraid, or otherwise anxious. Try to get to the heart of the matter and deal with the cause and not the symptoms.

- Be sure your child eats a healthy breakfast and gets enough sleep—low energy makes leaving the house very hard. Consider adding vitamins to your child's morning routine.

GET YOUR KID TO PUT ON SUNSCREEN

The sun is shining, and you are about to enjoy the beautiful day when the words "no sunscreen" come right out of your angel's mouth. A chase ensues. It's hard but true: Your child must be lathered up before your day can truly begin. Until a walk-in SPF shower or a sunscreen pill is on the market, you must do the work manually.

LAYING THE GROUNDWORK

- First and foremost, let your child know that this is not a choice. In order to go out in the sun, they must have on sunscreen.

- Plan to put on sunblock before you get to your final destination—ideally, when you're getting dressed or just about to leave the house. This way, sand or dirt won't get stuck in the lotion as you apply.

- Use your TV. With a good children's show in front of them, most kids won't even notice what you are doing to them.

- Let your child put it on by themselves—you can be their "helper" and rub it in.

- If you're headed to the beach and you have a difficult lotioner on your hands, consider purchasing a UV-proof bodysuit (sometimes called a "rash guard")—that way, you'll only have the face, hands, and feet to lotion up.

- Do everything in your power to ensure that the sunscreen does not get into your child's eyes. It is incredibly painful and will create a Pavlovian response whenever you reach for the bottle. Allow your child to hold tissues or a towel over their eyes during the application process.

- Don't refer to it as "sunblock." Call it "Magic Lotion" that will act as a "magic shield," protecting them from the sun.

- Pretend that the lotion can benefit your kid in some way: make them a better swimmer, totally invisible, incredibly strong, or give them some other sort of power.

- If you're using a white zinc oxide sunscreen, turn the process into an art project—on your child's body. Rub some lotion on your child's belly, then draw in it with your fingers before rubbing in the lotion. Let them do the same with you when you put on your sunscreen.

- Use a natural incentive, if it exists: "When you have sunscreen on, we can go to the beach." If the destination is undesirable, you may need to develop an unnatural incentive. "When you have sunscreen on, you can [PICK THE MUSIC IN THE CAR/READ A STORY BEFORE WE GO]."

- Purchase a washrag hand puppet (available at most mass merchandisers or department stores) and use it to apply the lotion. It's much more fun when the duck applies the lotion than when you do.

- Take a paintbrush and a small bowl with you to the beach or the picnic. Let your child dip the brush in the lotion and paint it onto their body by themself. You rub it in as they paint (and look out for missed spots).

A LITTLE SNEAKY

"Do you want me or Daddy to put on your sunblock?"

"Do you want to put on the pink lotion or the green lotion?"

"Should we start with your toes or your nose?"

"Should we paint a tiger or a shark on your belly?"

RUB A DUB DUB

To the tune of "Rub a Dub Dub, Three Men in a Tub."

Rub a dub dub
The lotion we rub
And who do we rub it on?
We rub it on you
And doodle-ee-doo
We'll rub it until it is gone!

Lotion Races

If you have two grown-ups and two kids, have the teams race against each other to see who can finish the sunscreening process first, without skimping. If there is just one child or just one adult, use the personal best model: See if you can beat your own time. Either way, have the child count out loud.

- Appeal to your child's rational side and their instinctive desire for self-preservation. Explain the negative effects of sun, focusing on the short-term pain of a sunburn.

- Sunscreen your child while they are buckled into a car seat or stroller. It usually isn't pretty, but it gets the job done.

Bonus Song:

LUBE YOUR ARM

To the tune of "Row, Row, Row Your Boat."

Lube, lube, lube your arm [LEG, FACE, ETC.]
Slick it up with cream
You'll be safe out in the sun
If you wear sunscreen

GOOD BEHAVIOR

GET YOUR KID TO MEET SOMEONE NEW

Meeting someone new can be terrifying for some children. Their shyness kicks in, and they are overwhelmed. At the same time, your embarrassment kicks in as your normally well-mannered and smiling child plants themself behind your right knee while a well-meaning adult booms out a welcoming greeting.

LAYING THE GROUNDWORK

- When you know a visitor is coming, prepare your child if you can. Show pictures of the guest, if possible, and talk up the visit.

- Take time to role-play meeting new people. You can play your child, and your child can play the stranger.

- Have simple expectations. If making eye contact is too much for your child, tell them to look at some other part of the person's face when greeting them.

PRETTY SNEAKY

- Act shy yourself—hide behind your child instead of letting them hide behind you. The sheer absurdity of the situation should make them laugh, and it may break the ice.

- Prepare the visitor ahead of time. Let them know to give your child some space when they first meet. If your child has a favorite food or if there's a particular present you know they'd love, give it to the visitor to present to your child.

A LITTLE SNEAKY

"Do you want to say 'hello' or 'hola'?"

"Do you want to shake hands or feet?"

"Do you want to ask them their name or how old they are?"

WHEN YOU MEET SOMEBODY NEW

To the tune of "When You're Happy and You Know It."
Sing this before and, if necessary, during any new social situation.

When you meet somebody new, say "Hello!"
(*wave*) "Hello!"

When you see someone you know, say "Hello!"
(*wave*) "Hello!"
When you meet somebody new
And they're being nice to you
When you meet somebody new, say "Hello!"
(*wave*) "Hello!"
When your _____ comes to visit, give a hug
(*give a hug*)
When your _____ comes to visit, give a hug
(*give a hug*)
Give your _____ a big hug
'Cause [SHE'S/HE'S/THEY'RE] filled with lots of love
When your _____ comes to visit, give a hug
(*give a hug*)

GAMES PARENTS PLAY

"Hello! Bonjour! Hola!" Day

This is a game you can play with your child that will not only help them become more outgoing, but will also teach them other languages. At the start of every day, using the chart on page 67 (or your own research), let your child decide what "Hello Day" it is that day.

Your child's objective is to say "Hello" in the daily language to as many people as they can throughout the day.

Hola	**Spanish**
Bonjour	**French**
Annyeong	**Korean**
Guten Tag	**German**
Shalom	**Hebrew**
Dos Vidanya	**Russian**
Ni Hao	**Chinese**

IF THEY'RE ON TO YOU

After you've left the situation, have a heart-to-heart with your child. Tell them that you know it's hard to meet new people or to see people you don't remember but that you expect them to learn how to do it, and next time they can try again. Have them tell you one new thing they will try to accomplish the next time, whether it's saying "hello," shaking hands, or coming out of hiding.

NOTE:
Never push your child to kiss or hug someone they don't know or don't feel comfortable with. This is a life lesson that shouldn't be upstaged by your desire to make Aunt Betty feel good.

GET YOUR KID TO WRITE A THANK-YOU NOTE

Imagine you're a kid: You wait all year for your birthday, and the holidays never seem to arrive fast enough. Nothing is more satisfying than ripping off that wrapping paper and making a mess right in front of everyone! But your excitement turns into dread as you look over at your mom and notice she's writing down who gave you what. You know that within minutes you'll hear those loaded words: "You know you have to write thank-you notes this week." What a present buzzkill!

Of course, as a parent, you want to raise kids who appreciate gifts and the people who give them. You want them to understand that people spent their hard-earned money to buy and send those gifts, and that a thank-you note is small way to recognize that effort.

LAYING THE GROUNDWORK

- Before the birthday, holiday, or gift-giving event, talk to your child about what is expected regarding personalized thank-yous. If note writing becomes part of family culture, it will be more difficult to rebel against.

- Make sure your child sees you sending your own thank-you notes, whether by mail or electronically. Have them help you write them, and make a deal to help with theirs.

- Involve your child by inviting them to organize the address book or school list, which will make the note-writing part of the process less stressful.
- Stock up on kid-friendly cards, as well as other fun materials (stamps, stickers, and the like), before the event.
- Incorporate thank-you note preparation into your next art project. A rainy-day craft could be to make homemade cards that can be used throughout the year.

- Stash fun stamps and ink pads to add a homemade touch to store-bought cards. Check the ink pads beforehand to make sure they haven't dried up.
- Don't let the process drag on for days or weeks. Prompt your child to send the notes quickly, so they don't dread the next time they have to write them.

"Do you want to go pick out some thank-you cards or make them yourself?"
"Do you want to make a multiple-choice thank-you note on the computer or write each one individually?"

IF THEY'RE ON TO YOU

Don't let them use or play with the present until they write a thank-you note for it. Pay to play, baby!

THE CHALLENGE:

GET YOUR KID TO LET YOU LEAVE

The plans have been made. You are finally getting a night out. Now you must make your great escape. The key to a clean getaway is to prepare your child and prepare your getaway plan.

LAYING THE GROUNDWORK

- Let them know in advance when you are going out. Use some sort of visual prop to help them mentally and emotionally prepare. Show them a calendar, make a countdown chart, or use a paper loop chain, taking away a loop each day. Your child's personality, experience with being left with caregivers, and age will dictate how far in advance of the date you let them know. Some children will become anxious with too much time; others need sufficient time to prepare.

- Normalize the experience by enlisting neighborhood kids or parents to talk about how great it is when they are home with a babysitter.

- Make sure your child knows who is going to take care of them. Ideally your child will have spent some time with the person before the momentous date.

- Let them know exactly what they are going to do with the sitter: "After dinner the sitter will read you a story, help you brush your teeth, and put you to bed."

- Let them know how and when you are going to say goodbye: "After a story and a hug, we are leaving." IMPORTANT: You must follow through with whatever you say. If you linger or cave in to "one more story," you give your child the message that you are uneasy with leaving. Though that may be the case, do not show it if you still plan on making your move.

- Write down instructions and important numbers for your babysitter so that questions can be answered with a phone call, not a visit from you.

- Make your getaway while your child is distracted and having fun—playing with the sitter, watching television, reading a book, or dancing around. To facilitate this, purchase a new toy or video and give it to the babysitter to use to distract your child.

- Be sure that when you say goodbye you do it positively, confidently, and quickly. Don't linger or look sad—simply say a quick goodbye, tell your child to have a great time, and remind them that you'll be back later.

- Put everything you need (keys, wallet, bowling ball) by the door or in your car ahead of time so that you can make a clean and quick getaway.

- Make up a story about a child whose parents went out for the night. Describe how the child was sad at first, and a little afraid—but then they had a great time with the babysitter. Talk at length about all the things they did together, and how fun it was. End with a note about how "as they said they would, the little kid's parents came home right on time, peeked in on their sleeping kid, kissed them on the cheek, and went to bed."

A LITTLE SNEAKY

"[NAME OF SITTER] is coming to have dinner with you tonight, so you can pick something special for dinner—what do you want?"

"Mommy and I are going out soon, but we can read one story or play one game together before we go—which do you want to do?"

"Do you want to give me a goodbye kiss or a goodbye hug?"

GOODBYE, MOMMY

To the tune of "Goodnight, Ladies." Sing this short goodbye song as you're hugging your child and saying goodbye. You can of course substitute whatever parent or guardian names are appropriate—Daddy and Papa, Mommy and Mama, Grandma and Grandpa, Erin and George, etc.

Goodbye, Mommy
Goodbye, Daddy
Goodbye, parents
I'll see you in my dreams

The Wave

After you've got your coat on and you've hugged your child, play "The Wave" to help make leaving fun. Simply put, you find funny ways of waving as you head toward the door. Ask your child to imitate you. Don't attempt to do more than three waves at any given departure—you'll have to linger too long.

WAVES TO TRY

- Through the legs

- Over your head

- Around your back

- With thumbs hooked, flapping like a bird

- With palms pressed together, opening and closing your hands like an alligator

- One-, two-, three-, four-, and five-finger waves

Through the legs

Bird

Alligator

Two-finger

IF THEY'RE ON TO YOU

Go out and have a blast anyway, leaving the babysitter to calm your child. Eventually, they will settle down. Besides, you need the night out, and your children will be happier if you are happier.

GET YOUR KID TO SLEEP OVER WITH FAMILY OR FRIENDS

The time has come. You need more than dinner and a movie; you need some quality time without the kids. You need a vacation. Whether your child will stay at home with someone else or spend the time away at a trusted adult's house, the trick is to involve them in the preparations, and make the time spent away from you special and fun.

LAYING THE GROUNDWORK

- Talk to your child about some special things that they can do with the caregiver. This might mean a trip to the zoo, baking cookies, or anything else that is special to your child.

- Tell your child exactly when you will call to check in. Make sure that you do! Let your child know that the caregiver knows how to get in touch with you.

- If they'll be staying away from home, pack up all their necessities so that they can see that their favorite cup and other comforting items will be going along. Make sure that the host has other familiar essentials: the right kind of milk or juice, their favorite fruits and snacks, and maybe even some food allowed only on special occasions.

- The more you can involve your child in packing, the better. Let them pick out their favorite clothes and toys to bring.

- Be sure to include a small photo album in your child's suitcase, just in case they need to have some "visiting time" with you.

- With your child's help, make a "sleepaway book" about what's going to happen while you are away. Include photos of whom they're going to stay with, where they'll be staying, and what they'll do. Have them draw pictures for the book as well, and look through the book several nights in a row before you go. By the time you leave, your child should be really clear about what to expect.

- Make a "sleepaway chart" that will let them keep track of how many days are left before the end of the trip. Give them stickers or a marker to check off the days at bedtime. They can also use this as a scrapbook to record memories of the time spent with the caretaker.

PRETTY SNEAKY

- Give the grandparents (or sitters) some leeway with bedtime, food, and any nonsafety issues. Make sure they feel free to show an extra episode of their favorite program, eat dinner in the den, or stay up a little later than usual to help make the experience fun for your child.

- Bribe your child: Buy a gift, wrap it, and put it in your child's suitcase. Show them the wrapped present, and tell them that they can open it only when they get to their destination.

A LITTLE SNEAKY

"Would you like to take your teddy bear or your bunny with you?"

"Which blanket do you want to take?"

"Would you like me to call in the morning when you wake up or at night before you go to sleep?"

"What special foods do you want to eat while I'm away?"

WE'RE GOING ON A SLEEPOVER

To the beat of "We're Going on a Lion Hunt."

We're going on a sleepover
We're gonna have a good time

I'm so glad
It's a wonderful thing!

We're gonna sleep at Grandma's
We're gonna play some new games
I'm so glad
It's a wonderful thing!

I'm gonna take my teddy bear
I'm gonna take my PJs
I'm so glad
It's a wonderful thing!

IF THEY'RE ON TO YOU

Even with the best prep, most children, at first, are going to be very sad when you leave and will do everything to keep you home. Give lots of hugs and kisses. Reinforce how much fun they will have and let them know when you will be in touch. Then, leave!

GET YOUR KID TO SIT STILL

Very young children have about a fifteen-minute attention span—so whenever any activity takes longer than that, they're likely to get restless. If this is their natural tendency, imagine how restless they'll become when they truly dislike the activity or are just plain not interested.

LAYING THE GROUNDWORK

- Never go to a place where your child will be asked to sit or stand still without a stash of books, paper, and crayons (or small noiseless toys) to keep your child occupied. Let them pick the books or the toys to take along.

- If they're going to have to remain seated for a really long time (for example, when traveling by car or plane), consider taking along a laptop or tablet to show movies.

- At restaurants, make your child sit in a high chair or booster seat and always strap them in. A captive audience is a good audience.

PRETTY SNEAKY

- If there's time, go to the playground or the park before you go anywhere that your kid will be required to sit or hold still—this will allow them to "run it off."

- Walk—don't drive or stroll—to your destination, if possible. This, too, will burn off energy.

- Cast a magic "freeze spell" on your child that lasts until the end of the event. Or at least until your child gets restless again—then have them cast the spell on you. Take turns.

A LITTLE SNEAKY

"Do you want to sit in the chair or on my lap?"

"Do you want to read or draw?"

"Do you want to stop running around now or after I count to ten?"

GAMES PARENTS PLAY

Statues

Teach your child how to play "Statues." Tell them you're going to time them to see how long they can stay completely still like a statue. Count the seconds (quietly). When they move, praise them for holding still for such a long time— then tell your child you want to see if they can "beat their own record."

IF THEY'RE ON TO YOU

You may have to simply bite the bullet and take your child out of the situation if things really get tough. Don't negotiate; just pick them up and go.

GET YOUR KID TO SURVIVE AN AIRPLANE TRIP

Leaving on a jet plane is always such a romantic notion—until the captain turns on the fasten seatbelt sign and your newly potty-trained toddler says they've gotta go. Or their ears start hurting. Or they just have to move around. No more gazing out the window or drifting off to sleep—traveling on an airplane with a young child is never relaxing.

> **NOTE:**
> Always pack extra clothes, diapers, and food in your carry-on in case of delays, accidents, or lost luggage.

LAYING THE GROUNDWORK

- Talk with your child in advance about expected plane behavior. Explain that they will have to sit still when you tell them to.

- Describe the duration of the flight in terms they will understand: The trip may take as long as "five *Sesame Streets*." Teach them about the fasten seatbelt sign so that they can watch it light up.

- Before you board, run around. Frolic in the airport until the last possible moment.

- If possible, place your child between you and your partner or seat your child in the window seat next to you so that they can't scoot away.

- Bring several of your child's favorite quiet toys, lots of books and coloring stuff, as well as a few new things to make the time go by. Play-Doh, a glowstick, or a mini flashlight can make for hours of entertainment. Give the new toys one at a time, so the process takes longer.

- If you'll be receiving a meal, request a kid's meal when booking your tickets. Even if your child doesn't eat the food, there may be fun packaging or a toy they can play with.

- To minimize the discomfort of pressure in the ears at takeoff and landing, get your child to suck and swallow by any means necessary. This may mean nursing, using a pacifier, drinking, eating, sucking a lollipop, or chewing gum, depending on your child's age.

- Charm the flight attendants when you board—their support will be useful if things get hairy. Be polite to your nearby seatmates as well—their patience will also come in handy.

PRETTY SNEAKY

- Load up your laptop, phone, or tablet with kid-friendly media and don't leave home without it. Though you may feel like a bad parent for plugging your child in, your fellow passengers will thank you. To avoid feeling too guilty, sneak in some education by downloading varied types of music, audiobooks, and nature documentaries, instead of hours of mindless animation.

- Using blankets, build your child a tent by draping the blanket over the back of their seat. This airplane tent is a great place to read and play (bring along a mini flashlight), and may even help your child shut the world out enough to fall asleep.

A LITTLE SNEAKY

"We have to stay in our seats, so do you want to play with _____, _____, or just read?"

"We can't get off the plane yet—should we go see if there are any kids to play with or just sit here and draw?"

FLYIN' ON AN AIRPLANE

To the tune of "Leaving on a Jet Plane."

All our bags are packed
We're ready to go
We're on the plane
We have Play-Doh
Already we're excited for the sky . . .

We're flyin' on an airplane
On Monday we'll be back again
How fun, we get to go . . .

Name That Cloud

Try to find characters, animals, people, shapes, letters, or numbers in the clouds.
Tell your child to find five things in the sky—then it's your turn.

When things get really dire and you have to do anything you can to calm your
little angel before the passengers revolt, head for the restroom with your child.
Sure, it's small, but at least you'll have some privacy.

THE CHALLENGE:

GET YOUR KID TO TALK QUIETLY

Let's face it—most children do not know the power of their own voice. Maybe it's that they spend the first year of life communicating only through crying and yelling, or maybe it's that they just don't understand the difference between tones. Either way, sooner or later, you're going to have to find a way to quiet your child.

LAYING THE GROUNDWORK

- Speak to your child in a normal tone of voice. Duh!

- Your child is most likely to yell when they are trying to get your attention and you are doing something else. Help your child understand that it's not appropriate to interrupt you when you're talking to someone else—that they simply need to wait or ask you what they want to ask you in a normal voice.

- Teach your child the difference between *quiet, normal,* and *loud.* Say, in a whisper, "This is a quiet voice." Make them repeat it in the same tone. Then say, in a normal tone, "This is a normal inside voice." Have them repeat it back. Then say, in a loud voice, "AND THIS IS LOUD!" Have your child repeat it. Do this over and over until they understand the differences. You can even have them sing a favorite song in a quiet voice, a normal voice, and a loud voice.

- When your child yells, don't tell them to simply "stop yelling." Say, "You don't need to yell—I can hear you when you use your normal voice." Teach your child when it's appropriate to be quiet (e.g., when their brother is napping), to use a normal voice (e.g., in a restaurant), and to use a loud voice (e.g., when they need help).

- Whisper to your child, and they'll usually whisper back.
- Tell your child that you can only hear requests spoken in a normal tone of voice.
- If you're in a situation in which you can't speak at all, have your child draw a picture of what they want or need, or point to it.

"You're such a good whisperer—let me hear you whisper that as quietly as you can."

"I know you can be really loud—but how quiet can you talk?"

GAMES PARENTS PLAY

The Wordless Game

Tell your child, in a quiet voice, that you're going
to play "The Wordless Game," and they're going
to have to ask their question without words. If, for
example, they want something to eat, tell your
child to point to themselves, then to mime eating
something. If your child wants a book to read,
tell your child to point to themselves, then to mime
reading, and so on. They get one point for every
wordless message they get across to you—and a
sticker or other small prize for every ten points.

IF THEY'RE ON TO YOU

Ignore them until they speak normally.

GET YOUR KID TO STOP CRYING

There are several tactics parents can master when attempting to get their child to stop crying, depending upon the cause of the tears. The key is figuring out which technique to use—and this depends on whether the crying is due to injury or frustration or is a form of manipulation. Changing your child's natural inclination to cry as a means of communication can be difficult—after all, for the first year or more it was the only available expression.

LAYING THE GROUNDWORK

- Consider teaching very young children (even as young as six months) a few key baby sign-language signs to communicate their needs. A few simple signs will not only empower your child to tell you what they really want or need, but will teach them that clear communication is the best means to their desired end, not crying or acting up.

SIGNS TO MASTER

- More
- Sleep
- Milk
- Water
- All done
- Food

More

Sleep

Milk

Water

All done

Food

It's easy to do—just perform each sign every time you use the associated word, and eventually, your child will pick it up. Be patient and watch carefully—the way your child performs the sign may not be exactly as you do it.

- Instead of telling your child to stop crying, say that you can't understand what they're saying, but if they use their words you'll be able to help.

- Let your child know that you feel their pain by acknowledging the cause of their trauma. "I know you really wanted to go to the park, but it's raining." "I know you want to run with these scissors, but it's not a good idea—you could get really hurt."

- If the crying is basically unfounded, it may be that your child is really saying that they're overtired or hungry.

PRETTY SNEAKY

- Master the art of misdirection. This is where new toys, puppets, and other distractions come in handy. Even an enthusiastic "Look at that tree!" might stop the flow of tears. If your child is crying because someone took something away from them, quickly replace the item with another one.

- If your child is crying because of a minor injury, pretend to "punish" the item that caused the injury. "Coffee table! How dare you hurt my baby! You need to apologize *right now*."

- If your child sustains a relatively minor injury (a bump on the head, a scrape on the knee), you can often stop the crying by reenacting the "crime." This can get you a laugh and stop residual crying after you've initially comforted your child. Pretend to investigate the cause of the incident by saying, "Now how did you fall? You were running like this . . ." (Run the same path as your child.) "When you tripped over a stick like this . . ." (Pretend to trip, then fall.) "Then you cried like this." (Cry in an exaggerated and amusing manner.) It should defuse the situation and make your child laugh.

- Perform physical humor by reenacting the incident in a funny way, pretending that you didn't see the initial injury. "My poor baby! You fell— now how did you do tha—whoooaaaa! (CRASH) Ow—that *did* hurt!" There's nothing funnier to a child than seeing their parent fall.

"Do you want me to go over and have a talk with the sidewalk you fell on?"
"Do you want to tell me why you're so upset, or do you want me to guess?"
"Did you get hurt, or did you get scared?"

IF YOU'RE SAD AND YOU KNOW IT

To the tune of "If You're Happy and You Know It." Singing the following song, when accompanied with a comforting hug and kiss, can calm your child and distract them at the same time.

If you're sad and you know it
Give a cry
If you're sad and you know it
Give a cry
If you're sad and you know it
And you really want to show it
If you're sad and you know it
Give a cry

Use the following variations if applicable to your situation.

If you're hurt and you know it
Rub your [INJURED BODY PART]

If you're mad and you know it
Stomp your feet (*stomp your feet*)

If you're tired and you know it
Go to sleep (*make snoring sounds*)

If you're grumpy and you know it
Say HARUMPF!

If you're crazy and you know it
Go like this (*do something silly*)

IF THEY'RE ON TO YOU

- Popsicles and lollipops cure all ills.
- Let them cry—sometimes, kids just need to get over it by themselves. This is especially true when they cry for no good reason.

GET YOUR KID TO STOP WHINING

Whining: It's a time-honored kid communication tactic, and one of the most annoying things parents have to deal with. Why do kids do it? Partially, it's to play on your emotions. They know you react to their crying, so whining about something is a more moderate version of an extreme solution. To stop this, you'll need ways to firmly point out that whining isn't acceptable, and that there are better ways to ask for things.

LAYING THE GROUNDWORK

- At an early stage, teach your child how to politely ask for things—that saying "please" is more effective than whining or crying. Praise them when they do this well: "Thank you for asking so nicely."

- Firm statements or commands like "Stop whining" are usually ineffective. Try saying, "Sweetie, just ask—you know I don't like it when you whine." The old standby phrase "Use your words" comes in handy here.

- Teach your child to be self-sufficient: "If you want something, go and get it yourself if you can."

- Don't respond in a frustrated or angry tone—this is simply the adult version of the behavior you're trying to fix.

- Teasingly whine back. Say, "You know I don't like it when you whine. What if I always asked you to do something by whining? (*switch to a whining voice*) We have to get going now, why won't you come put on your coat. I really, really want you to put on your coat . . ." The reality of their behavior, coupled with the absurdity of their parent whining, should make them realize how silly it is.

- Pretend that the whining is actually a small animal that's making noise somewhere. "Hey! Did you hear that? That whining noise? It sounds like it's coming from you but it can't be—you know not to whine when you're asking for something. I'm sure you'd say please and ask in a normal voice, so there must be a baby cow or puppy somewhere—maybe it's in your pocket. Let's look." The message should come across loud and clear.

"I don't understand you very well when you whine—say it again in a normal voice."

"Maybe you should try singing it—the whining isn't going to work."

The Whining Jar

1. Take a small jar and label it "The Whining Jar." Have your child draw on the label to involve them in the process.

2. Place ten or twenty small items that your child likes in the jar—stickers, rubber balls, plastic animals.

3. Explain to your child that for every day that passes without any whining they will get to pick an item from the jar.

4. Replenish the jar when it gets low.

IF THEY'RE ON TO YOU

Never give in or yield to a whine just because you're tired of hearing it—you will send your child the message that whining is an acceptable way to get what they want. Ignore the whining until they get tired of their own voice and stop.

GET YOUR KID TO STOP THROWING A TANTRUM

Nearly all children between the ages of one and three have temper tantrums, because they want to test the limits of your patience and their control, or because they can't use words to fully express their emotions and frustrations. Give them the tools to do this, and they will not throw a fit as often.

LAYING THE GROUNDWORK

- Teach your child to use words to express their feelings. When a tantrum occurs, say, "I don't understand what you want when you're crying like this— take a few deep breaths and tell me."

- Whenever possible, involve your child in decision making—if not about what to do, then at least how to do it. For example, they don't get to decide whether or not to take a bath; they get to decide whether it's a bubble bath or what toys to take.

- Always give your child ample warning when changing activities. Since kids have no real concept of time, saying "we're leaving in five minutes" may not be meaningful. Instead, try, "We're leaving at the end of this song."

PRETTY SNEAKY

- Use the art of distraction. Make a silly face, pretend to fall, do a funny dance—whatever you have to do to divert attention from their misery.

- If you have a doll or puppet with you or nearby, talk to the child in the doll's or puppet's voice. For a child, sometimes talking to a "peer" and explaining how upset they are is easier and more comforting than talking to a parent.

- Change the scene. Taking a child into a restroom, outside a store, or back to your car usually gets them to calm down.

- Get your child to take several slow, deep breaths—into a paper bag if they've really lost control.

- Unless they're really misbehaving (hitting, kicking, throwing things, or screaming uncontrollably), try ignoring them.

A LITTLE SNEAKY

"Do you want to stay longer and calm down or just go now?"

"I can't understand you when you're like this—do you want to try to tell me what's wrong or just show me?"

SUPER FREAK

To the tune of "Superfreak."

She's a very freaky girl
The kind who cannot get her words out
She's the kind of kid who'd rather throw a tantrum
And collapse right at your feet

She's a very freaky girl
The kind who really is upset now
She's the kind of kid who needs some good attention
To get her off the street

She's a superfreak, superfreak
She's super freaky

Don't punish your child for a temper tantrum—rather, work on giving them the skills to use words to express their needs and emotions more clearly.

GET YOUR KID TO PUT SOMETHING DOWN

Once a child gets a hold of something they really want, you'll be hard pressed to get them to let go of it without some parental trickery. As a result, you should be prepared with an array of cons and redirections when shopping or visiting with friends.

LAYING THE GROUNDWORK

- Whenever you go to the store, explain that you have to pay, with money, for the items you are buying. That way, your child won't think it's all for the taking. And resist buying things for your child on an impulse. Seeing you do this will make them think it's to be expected.

- Rather than forbidding your child to touch breakable items, let them hold anything they want—for a prenegotiated length of time. "Yes—you can hold the ceramic duck, but you need to put it back after we're done paying." This will prevent them from seeing such items as forbidden fruit.

- When in a store with your child, keep them in the cart as much as you can—that way, you can more easily control their impulses. As you shop, allow them to hold the items you're going to buy; don't let them run around pulling things randomly off the shelves. These items will seem essential to your child.

- Master the art of the swap: "No, you can't have that—can you hold [MY PURSE/YOUR DOLL/THIS ITEM] instead?"
- When shopping, let your child pick one item that they can "buy," saying, "You can pick one small toy to buy from this section—which do you want?" Or, "We can't buy that toy, but we can get a book—let's go over to the book section so you can choose one."
- Redirect their attention: "We can't play with that right now—but I really want to play catch with you later. Will you go pick a ball to play with?"
- Rather than simply taking the item away, involve your child by getting them to put the item away or give it back.
- Tell your child that they can't take the item home, but that when you get home you will make them a "present list" and make sure that item is on it. That way, everyone will know what to get them for their next birthday.

A LITTLE SNEAKY

"Do you want to put the stuffed animal back or should I?"

"We don't have enough money for that—but you can pick _____ instead."

GAMES PARENTS PLAY

Where Does This Go?

Tell your child exactly what you're going to get in the store and that you're not going to buy anything else. Then ask them if they want to play the "Where Does This Go?" game. As you're walking through the store, your child can pick up to three items to hold during the shopping trip—make it clear from the outset that these are not items to keep. When you've finished your shopping, tell your child, "Now we need to see how fast we can put these things back—do you remember where they went? Ready, set, GO!" Count the seconds and keep track of the time it takes for them to direct you to the appropriate location. Remember the time for future shopping trips, and challenge your child to beat their old time. Reward them for having successfully returned the items each time, with the honor of paying the clerk or receiving a sticker or a snack.

PUT THE STUFF BACK

To the tune of "Hit the Road, Jack." Sing the following song while you are walking around the store (or house) putting back the items your child has collected during your visit.

Put the stuff back
Take it out of the sack
Let's go
Let's go
Let's go
Let's go

Put the stuff back
Take it out of the sack
Let's go

WHAT'D YOU SAY?

Put the stuff back
Right on the stack
Let's go
Let's go
Let's go
Let's go

Put the stuff back
Right on the stack
Let's go

WHAT'D YOU SAY?

Oh baby, oh baby
I treat you so mean
I'm the meanest old [MOMMY/DADDY]
That you've ever seen
But you know
If I say so
We've got to put back all our things and go

THAT'S RIGHT!

Put the stuff back
Don't give me no flack
No more
No more
No more
No more

Put the stuff back
Don't give me no flack
No more

IF THEY'RE ON TO YOU

Grabbing the item out of your child's hands is pretty much a sure path to a temper tantrum. Simply say firmly (but not angrily), "OK, you need to put that back after I count to ten." This method simply tells them that they can hold the item a bit longer (and gives them a timeframe they can comprehend), but it isn't so high-pressured or threatening as to cause a tantrum.

AROUND THE HOUSE

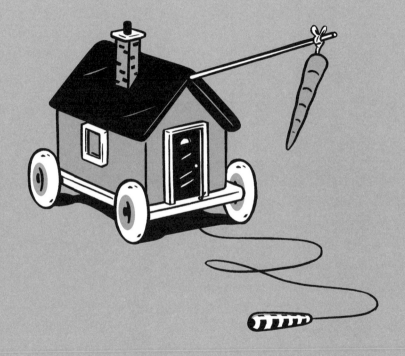

GET YOUR KID TO SHARE

We tell children to share as if it were the most natural thing in the world. But if sharing were so natural, wouldn't the world be a different place? It is therefore highly unrealistic to think that a toddler will, of their own free will, share their possessions on a regular basis. A child must believe that sharing is expected, necessary, and even beneficial. Parents must be the ones to set the good example.

LAYING THE GROUNDWORK

- Read lots of stories about sharing to your child. Make up some of your own. Acknowledge that it is often hard to share but that sharing brings intrinsic rewards (praise by parents, fun with friends, etc.).

- Whenever possible, have multiples of things (two similar trucks, two pens, two pads of paper, two dolls).

- Hype it up whenever your child does share. Praise, praise, praise. Though your child should know this is expected behavior, they should feel good about doing it.

- If a playmate is coming over, put away all "special toys." Ask your child which few toys will be just too hard to share and honor their decision. Stow them in a closet and assure your child that their playmate will have no access. This sets the stage for informing your child in no uncertain terms that you expect that they will share everything else. This is a "speak now or forever hold your peace" situation.

- Never let your child take an item to school or to a friend's house that they aren't willing to share.

- Although children don't easily grasp the concept of sharing, they can easily understand "taking turns." "First, Sydney gets to play with the guitar—then it's your turn."

- Trick your child into "trading," which is really the same as cross-kid sharing: "Why don't you trade for a while? You can play with the magic wand for now, and Avery can play with the fire engine."

- Have at your disposal a sheet of stickers or a "cool" stamp. Tell your child and their playmates that you are the "Sharing Fairy." When you see someone sharing, that person will get a sticker or a stamp to show everyone what a good job they are doing.

"Should your friend get the first turn with the blocks or with the dolls?"

"What toys do you want to take to Cooper's house to share today?"

"Do you want to give Olive a turn on the bike now or in a few minutes?"

GAMES PARENTS PLAY

Musical Toys

For children who have a tough time sharing, this variation on musical chairs can make the concept more fun. The principle is the same:

1. When the music starts, every child is handed a toy to play with.

2. Everyone sits or stands in a circle, playing with their toy until the music stops.

3. When you stop the music, the children put down their toys and move one spot to the right.

This way, everyone gets a chance to play with all the toys.

IF THEY'RE ON TO YOU

- Validate your child's feelings—"I can see by the look on your face that you are upset. It is really hard to share, and it can be really frustrating."

- Identify the problem—"It looks like you both want the yellow truck, but Jane had it first."

- Give two choices (unless they are older and can come up with a variety on their own)—"We could take turns. First Sophie can have the truck and Max can play with the police car, and then you could switch. Or Sophie could play with the police car while Max plays with the truck, and then you could switch."

- If the children simply can't share a toy, remove it and encourage the children to play with the other toys. If one child is the problem, yanking a toy away from someone else repeatedly, that child should be removed from the situation. It isn't pretty, but it does work.

THE CHALLENGE:

GET YOUR KIDS TO STOP ANNOYING EACH OTHER

Even our favorite fake TV families had their share of annoyances—Carol and Mike Brady certainly had to step in from time to time to resolve a heated Brady kid squabble. And so it is in real life: Siblings and friends can frequently drive each other crazy. When do you referee? When do you let them work it out? It is not an easy job to maintain harmony—but it is the job you signed up for.

LAYING THE GROUNDWORK

- Decide what your own ground rules are going to be, then stick to them. Try to be consistent about when you will intervene. Will you only intervene if it is a safety issue, or will you mediate every conflict? Do you expect your kids will need your help to work most things out, or do you expect they will do it on their own?

- When your child comes to you, usually crying or whining, complaining that "David won't leave me alone" or "Kelly keeps calling me a baby," don't take matters into your own hands—teach your child how to confront the situation on their own. "Why don't you tell David to stop?" "Why don't you tell Kelly how that makes you feel?"

- Make sure the offending sibling or friend isn't simply hungry. Low blood sugar can make anyone prone to angry outbursts. Feed the kids if this might be the case.

- Set up a "cooperative area" or "neutral zone." In this area, all children are obliged to obey the nonnegotiable rules of play: respect each other, talk reasonably, listen to each other, and do not push or hit. The zone is magical, and all must follow its enforced ethic of "peace on earth and good will toward all." If a child can't follow the rules of this tiny magical kingdom, they must leave the area until they can follow directions. (Make sure that the best toys are located in the cooperative area.)

- Give siblings spaces that are completely their own, especially if they share a room. Let them know that if they need alone time, they can go to their special place. This "special place" can be a tiny nook somewhere in the house (e.g., a closet, a corner, etc.), as long as it is only theirs.

- If things are really tough, delegate chores. Give them each their own "job"— in separate areas of the house, preferably—and put them to work.

A LITTLE SNEAKY

"Do you want to stop annoying your sister, or do you want to leave the room?"

"Are you and your brother able to work this out on your own, or do you need my help?"

"I know you don't like it when people bother you—so what would you like to do instead?"

GAMES PARENTS PLAY

Walk a Mile in Each Other's Shoes

Play a game in which, for a set period of time, each sibling must pretend to be the other. You might even have them trade shirts or shoes to facilitate the role play. The main rule is that making fun of the other person is strictly forbidden. The point of the game is to really try to imagine what it is like to be the other person. Give lots of direction so that each sibling gets to really feel how their annoying behaviors impact the other person.

IF THEY'RE ON TO YOU

Sell them on some outdoor time. It may be less than ideal outside, but gear them up as best you can and find somewhere for them to frolic. Since no one "owns" the great outdoors (or the neighborhood park), it is neutral territory.

GET YOUR KID TO HELP WITH CHORES

Ever since Cinderella, chores have gotten a bad rap—only wicked parents make you do them. In real life, we all have our chores to do. They make us feel as if we are important members of the family and community. For kids, this abstract feeling can become a very real source of pride as long as you praise and reward them accordingly.

LAYING THE GROUNDWORK

- Explain why you are making them do the chore(s). No, it is not to torture them, whatever they may believe. It is to share the family work load, offer an opportunity to contribute to the family, help teach responsibility, and instruct in housekeeping skills.

- Set up reasonable expectations. Don't expect your two-year-old to peel vegetables for dinner (but also don't assume that your five-year-old can't). According to research, here's what your youngster is capable of:

TWO- TO THREE-YEAR-OLDS

- Pick up toys and put them in the proper place.
- Sweep the floor.

- Set the table with napkins, plates, and silverware.

- Clear their own place after eating.

- Unload utensils from the dishwasher (except things like sharp knives).

FOUR-YEAR-OLDS

Everything the younger kids can do, plus:

- Feed pets on a regular schedule.

- Help do yard work.

- Dust the furniture.

- Prepare cold cereal.

- Get the mail.

- Help wash the dishes or fill the dishwasher.

FIVE-YEAR-OLDS

Everything the younger kids can do, plus:

- Make their bed.

- Clean their room.

- Scrub the sink, toilet, and bathtub.

- Fold clean clothes and put them away.

- Help clean out the car.

- Take out the garbage.

- Take the time to train your child to do what is expected of them. Your children want to feel capable and competent—give them the tools to do so. The up-front investment in chores is nothing compared to the lifetime return.

- In order to get your child more invested in chores, and to understand the need for them, ask them to help you brainstorm a list of all the things that make your household run. Prompt them if they are missing key chores: "How do your dirty clothes make it from your bedroom floor back to your drawer, clean?" "How do your toys end up back in your toy box?"

- Set aside a "chore time" when everyone works at once. This allows for more supervision and also more fun.

PRETTY SNEAKY

- Provide kid-sized equipment whenever possible. A small broom and dustpan or a tiny rake can inspire wonders.

- Don't call them "chores"—say that your child is being your "Special Assistant." A badge or hat to help them play this role can provide extra incentive.

- Whenever possible, work to music. Playing the same album every time you do a certain chore can reinforce the message that it's fun and that it's time to work.

- Give your child lots of praise and thanks for their contribution to the family.

- Use "As soon as _____, then _____" to ensure chores get done. For example, "As soon as you make your bed, you can play outside."

- Use chore charts and incentives. Each day a child completes a chore, they get a sticker or a star on the chart. When they have accrued five, ten, or fifteen stars (set the amount beforehand), they can earn something special. This "something special" can be anything from time with a parent doing whatever they want to an allowance, a new toy, or another desired prize.

> **NOTE:**
> If the work isn't perfect, never redo it in front of your child. Do it better later, or keep your sense of humor: If a child forgets to set plates on the table, pretend to serve dinner right on the table. Your child will get the hint and get a giggle out of it, too.

A LITTLE SNEAKY

"Do you want to put away your toys first or make your bed first?"

"I am going to pick up all your socks: What are you going to pick up, your pants or shirts?"

"Do you want to do your chore before your homework or after?"

"When you complete your chore, do you want to play on the computer or watch a video?"

I'VE BEEN WORKIN' WITH MY FAMILY

To the tune of "I've Been Workin' on the Railroad."
Sing the following tune whenever you're working to make the job more fun. There's a reason railroad workers sang—it helped to pass the time.

I've been workin' with my family
All the livelong day
I've been working with my family
Just to help in every way

Can't you see my Mama smilin'
Smilin' since the day I was born?
Can't you see my Daddy beamin'
He's proud night till morn.

Gonna help my Mom
Gonna help my Mom
Gonna help my Mom each day-ay-ay
Gonna help my Dad
Gonna help my Dad
Gonna help my Dad each day.

Chore-Picking Games

These games provide a fair and simple way to divide chores among children in your family or among children and adults. Choose the version of the game that is most appropriate to your family's style and the ages of your children. The games ensure that no one (other than perhaps a parent) is stuck with the same chore for a very long time.

CHORE WHEEL

For three- to four-year-olds. Find or draw pictures that represent different communal chores, such as putting away the silverware or setting the table. (Leave out individual chores like making the bed if everyone is expectated to make their bed in the morning.)

Make a wheel out of a sturdy paper plate or a circle made out of heavy construction paper. Place the pictures of the chores around the edge of the wheel. Make a cardboard arrow as a spinner, and use a brad to fasten it to the center of the wheel. Let your kids spin the wheel to determine what chores they will do for that day or week. Write the chores down on a chore chart as a reminder and to build in incentives.

CHORE RAFFLE

For four- to six-year-olds. Write each chore on a piece of paper and put the pieces of paper into a box with a lid. (Customize separate boxes with age-appropriate chores if your kids are different ages.) Once a week, each child picks one or two chores out of the box, which they will do for the week. Write the chores down on a chore chart to keep track.

IF THEY'RE ON TO YOU

Have clear consequences discussed up front. Your child should know what happens if they decide not to set the table or make the bed. Simple, immediate, and natural consequences are best. For example, if your child does not pick up their toys at the end of the day, they may not play with them the next day.

GET YOUR KID TO CLEAN UP

Before having children, you might have said, "My place is a mess" when there were a couple of dishes in the sink. Now, "My place is a mess" means that there are toys everywhere, the dirty breakfast dishes are making friends with the dirty dinner dishes, and the dirty laundry is threatening a revolt. Have reasonable expectations—homes with small children will always be a little dirtier and a little more cluttered. The trick is: How can you engage your children to be a part of the solution?

LAYING THE GROUNDWORK

- Let your child play with only a few things at a time so that cleanup is not overwhelming.

- Create a routine around cleanup. Maybe it always happens after dinner but before dessert. Or maybe it happens Saturday morning before anything "more fun" can start. Whatever schedule you choose, be consistent, build in an incentive, and start as young as possible.

- Make a simple visual chart of what you expect from cleanup. Show your child how to do each task before you expect them to try it. Make a copy of the chart so that they can check off each task as they complete it.

- Give a five-minute warning before cleaning up. Some kids may need an actual countdown.

- Be as specific as possible. Don't say "We need to clean up the playroom." Ask your child to put the blocks back in the box and put the box on the shelf, for example.

PRETTY SNEAKY

- If your child goes to school or daycare, find out their cleanup routines and mimic them at home. (At most schools, cleanup occurs after an activity is completed.)

- Institute a "five-minute cleanup" every day: after mealtime, select a song (take turns picking) and play it while everyone cleans up one part of the house.

- If you have multiple children, or are attempting to clean up with a group of children, have them line up and pass the items from child to child along the line until they reach their proper home.

- Don't let your child leave a room messy. Establish a pattern in which a room must be tidied up

before leaving. Turn it into a little melodrama—close the door and become a wizard who casts a spell on your child and who won't let them leave until the room is picked up.

- Make sure that everything being cleaned up has a set place to go. Whenever possible, label drawers and boxes with words and pictures so that cleanup is also a learning activity. Have a bin for random stuff— otherwise things stay cluttered, or items get misplaced.

- Praise, praise, praise—even if only a few items were cleaned up.

A LITTLE SNEAKY

"Do you want to clean up the blocks or the paints?"

"Do you want to listen to music while we clean or just sing a song?"

"Do you want to be the picker-upper or the putter-awayer?

THE CLEANUP SONG

To the tune of "It's Raining." Sing the following song relentlessly until the room is clean, the toys are picked up, or you just can't take it anymore:

Clean up
Clean up
Everybody clean up
We've got to put the _____ away
So everybody clean up.

GAMES PARENTS PLAY

The Cleanup Olympics

Tell your kids that, rather than simply cleaning up today, you're going to hold "The Cleanup Olympics." Create Olympic-esque event names like "Play Room Relay" or "Dishwasher Derby" or "My Room Pickup Sprint"—that will make it sound more compelling. You will be the judge, your kids the participants. Announce the event like a commentator: "Ava is stepping right into the living room, Tim, and she's ready to pick up all the things she left there this weekend. It's going to be tough for her—this isn't her favorite event—but she's trained long and hard for this. Question is, can she come out ahead of the Russian competitor who lives in the room down the hall?" Keep the commentary running throughout the cleanup, and at the end give your child a "score" and a ranking. If they like the game, keep a record of their best time or score, and have them attempt to "beat" their score at the next Cleanup Olympic games!

Variation: Tell your child that you're going to play "Scavenger Hunt." Ask them if they can find all the toys that are orange and put them away. Then move on to all the toys that have wheels, all the toys that are animals, all the toys that make noise, and so on until everything is put away. The "prize" can be anything from a sticker to a snack to just being allowed to leave the room.

IF THEY'RE ON TO YOU

- After your child has a chance to put their belongings away and they don't do it, put the clutter in a box. For your child to get those items back, they will need to do extra chores around the house. Don't make this a punishment; treat the process as simply the way things work to make a house run well.

- Purge. Sort through the toys with your child. Discard broken ones. Share some of the others with children who do not have enough toys (e.g., donate them to a local shelter). Make it a lesson on sharing and thankfulness, and reduce the amount of potential clutter.

THE CHALLENGE:

GET YOUR KID TO LIMIT SCREEN TIME

Kids love to watch shows, play games, and generally spend time on computers, TVs, tablets, phones, and any device they can get their hands on. Screen time isn't necessarily bad in and of itself—some of those shows are pretty educational!—but every expert agrees that it should be limited. Fortunately, many kids love screen time so much that you can very effectively (and sneakily) use it as a carrot for getting them to cooperate with babysitters, do chores, get in the car, or any number of other desirable outcomes.

LAYING THE GROUNDWORK

- Make sure your child knows they have a limited amount of screen time every day or week. Adjust the amount to your lifestyle, but we suggest no more than thirty minutes per day.

- Set a timer and train your child to realize that when the timer rings, the screen is turned off or the device is put away.

- Don't leave your phone or tablet lying around—make sure your child returns them to you or to a designated storage spot at the end of screen time. This will reduce temptation. If it's in the budget, buy a specific device for your child's screen time, like a low-cost tablet. This allows you to add a protective case, put parental controls on apps, and ensure that the device is returned to a specific place when screen time is over and not removed again until your child has permission. And it spares you the whining of a kid who wants you to hand over your phone!

- Consider guiding kids toward shows and games that have been adapted from books, or that have a book tie-in. When their screen time is up, offer the book instead.

- Don't let your child eat while watching a show. This creates an association with meals that can be hard to break.

PRETTY SNEAKY

- Make "screen bucks" out of paper or cardboard, explaining to your child that they will earn one buck each time they do something important (chores, reading, homework—whatever you choose). Make a buck worth fifteen or thirty minutes of screen time—the shorter the better, because they can earn more and use less!

- Allow your kid to use devices only when the batteries are low—that way, when the power runs out, their time runs out, too!

- Have the next activity ready to go when it's time to put devices away—the more time there is to wait, the more time there is to complain. When you start the timer, verbally prepare them for what's next: "Remember, it's dinnertime after your show's over. What do you want to drink?" "Should I get out the finger paints or watercolors when you're done with this game?"

- Tell your child that the device is "tired" and needs to rest for the night.

- If your child doesn't understand why you're allowed to play with your phone and they're not, let them read some of your work emails so they can see how boring it is.

- Use the desire for screen time to motivate your child to do other, less-desirable things first.

"Would you rather play on the computer by yourself, or play a board game with all of us?"

"We're leaving in fifteen minutes. You can watch until then, but only if you're ready to head out the door when I say it's time."

Hide the devices your kid uses to watch shows or play games and say they're broken and being fixed. You probably can't keep them away from screens forever, but a week or two of detox might do wonders. (If the devices are shared among the whole family, make sure you don't let your kid see you using them during this time!)

GET YOUR KID TO PLAY ALONE

Play is the most important daily activity for all children—it helps them to enjoy life, interact with others, experience new things, and learn. But why don't they ever want to play without you? Sure, some children do—industrious types who relish time alone amidst the toy detritus—but perhaps you didn't get one of those kids. Perhaps your child constantly wants your attention, your interaction, your fun. Who do they think they are, your dependent?

LAYING THE GROUNDWORK

- The key to increasing the odds that your child will play by themselves for any period of time is to be realistic about your expectations. If you think that you will make a four-course meal, do your laundry, write your dissertation, and catch up with a colleague today, you are in for disappointment. Be happy with a few moments of solace.

- Whenever your child plays by themself, even for a few moments, hype the fact that they are doing something special and "grown up."

- Make sure that there are toys for your child to play with everywhere in the house.

- If your child ever does play by themself, pay attention to which toys they choose—does it naturally happen with art supplies, small cars, or blocks? When you need your child to play alone, have those toys on hand.

PRETTY SNEAKY

- Encourage your child to play at the same thing you're trying to do. If you are making dinner, make the kitchen table their "cooking" area, complete with a mixing bowl, "ingredients" (you may need to forfeit some old rice or flour to this endeavor), and loads of utensils. If you are working on the computer, set them up with an old laptop or a shoebox you have tailored to look like one.

- Play music—it soothes the savage beast, and it distracts the needy child.

- Set up a "toy testing area," with five to ten toys for your child to play with on their own. Explain that you need them to play with each of the toys to decide which ones they like best.

- Tell your child that you have to do some work, but that you'll "get them started" on whatever they want to play with. Or, do something time-limited before you set them off on their own—read a story or sing a song.

- Set up a tent or a fort for your child. Kids love to crawl in and out, and the secluded nature of a fort will prevent your child from noticing that you're not playing with them. Place lots of toys and books inside, and give them a flashlight for better exploration.

- Give your child a clear play objective to accomplish, one that will take a bit of time: "Can you build me a castle? See how high you can go!" or "Will you draw a picture for Grandma?"

A LITTLE SNEAKY

"Why don't you teach your [SIBLING/DOLLS/STUFFED ANIMALS] how to play
_____ ?"

"You need to play on your own for a while—do you want me to set up the art supplies on this table or that table?"

"I have to make dinner, but I'll read you one story either before or after. Do you want to hear it now or later?"

GAMES PARENTS PLAY

The Play Station Course

Set up the room as an obstacle course full of different "play stations," with a task at each one that your child has to complete on their own. Explain that the objective isn't to do the tasks quickly, but rather to do each one well. Set up the following stations:

- Play-Doh station

- Blocks or Lego station

- Paint station

- Water station (with bowls, tubs, boats, ducks)

- Singing station (with music and microphone)

Make sure you create a path with barriers that they need to go over, under, or through in order to get to the next station.

IF THEY'RE ON TO YOU

For any of these tricks to work, you'll have to be prepared to be unavailable to play all the time. Let your child know that you are busy doing your job and that their job is to play. Tell them you will join in later and to get started without you. If you tell them you will check on them in a few minutes (you can set a timer if needed), make sure you do, so that your word is reinforced.

MEALTIME
AND
BEDTIME

GET YOUR KID TO EAT

When it comes to food, kids are at their most cunning. One night they act as if they haven't eaten all day, wolfing down the macaroni and cheese; the next they act as though they've just sipped a bad bottle of wine, unceremoniously spitting it out on the floor. Perhaps it's because eating is one thing kids can effectively resist. You can force them to get dressed, or to get into the car, or to get into the bath through sheer strength and will, but if they truly don't want to eat, you can't force food down their throats.

LAYING THE GROUNDWORK

- Give your child a choice of meals. There's never any guarantee, but they may be more likely to eat a meal that they've asked for.

- Don't fight the food battle. Your child will not starve themself—get comfortable with this fact, and let them decide whether they're hungry or not.

- Take your child to the housewares store and let them pick out a special placemat, bowl, dish, fork, spoon, and cup. They'll be more likely to use items they've chosen themself.

- Remember that most children have very short attention spans—usually not much more than fifteen minutes. If the meal is going to take longer than that, you'll need to entertain them. Negotiate a deal—"You eat, and I'll read."

- It's a bad idea to eat while watching television, but listening to music during the meal is fine. Let your child pick the tunes.

- Let your child taste things as you make them, telling them that you need their taste buds to make sure dinner tastes good.

- Have your child hold the dinner timer and give them the responsibility of telling you when it beeps.

- When the meal is ready, have your kid help serve or set the table. They will feel empowered and proud, and should be more willing to eat the food.

- If your child insists on having ice cream or cookies or some other dessert instead of dinner, try to cut a deal. Sometimes, the old "dinner first, then ice cream" negotiation won't work, so if you have a reasonable child on your hands, you might try the "one bite of dinner, one bite of ice cream" deal instead.

- Don't feed your child a meal away from the table—while they stand, while in the bath, while sitting in your lap before bed. While "seagulling" (swooping in for one bite at a time while running around) may get food into your child's body, it doesn't teach great table manners.

PRETTY SNEAKY

- Cut the food into friendly shapes—squares, triangles, circles, stars. Use cookie cutters for speed and efficiency.

- Arrange the food to look fun—like favorite characters, animals, faces, or scenes.

- Rename the foods. Be creative: Broccoli isn't broccoli, it's "baby trees." Chicken nuggets aren't chicken nuggets, they're "crunchy rocks." Other suggestions:

Carrots (when cut into circles)	"Orange Suns"
Carrots (when cut into sticks)	"Magic Wands"
Mashed Potatoes	"White Mud"
Cauliflower	"Baby White Trees"
Salad	"Rabbit Food"
Fish Sticks	"Fishing Rods"
String Cheese	"Spider Webs"

- Serve the food in a nontraditional way—don't simply put it on the plate. Give them fruit on a skewer (teach them to take off each piece by hand), or build a carrot log cabin. Use your imagination.

- Serve small portions in easy-to-eat bites. Portions that are too large—needing to be cut up or bitten off—may be unwieldy and instead will inspire them to play with the food (or shove it off the plate) rather than eat it.

- Get your child to help you make the meal. Give them an apron or cook's hat to wear. Ask them to hold things for you, stir things, season things. (Give your child premeasured liquids or seasonings to add.) Have them press the buttons of any device you need to operate (the blender, the toaster).

- Play "The Wishing Game." For every bite your child takes, they get to make a wish.

- Employ "puppet pressure": Feed your child while wearing a hand puppet. It's an amazing phenomenon—children often comply with a puppet's requests when they won't comply with yours.

A LITTLE SNEAKY

"Should we read or just tell stories and talk while we eat?"
"Which of your stuffed animals should we invite to lunch today?"
"Do you want to eat your pasta or your fruit salad first?"

FIVE LITTLE BROCCOLIS

To the beat of "Five Little Monkeys."

Five little broccolis
Sitting on a plate
One jumped off (*pick up one*)
And then got ate! (*place it in your child's mouth*)
The kid says "Yummy! That tastes great!
Is there any more broccoli on my plate?"

Four little broccolis
Sitting on a plate
One jumped off (*pick up one*)
And then got ate! (*place it in your child's mouth*)
The kid says, "Yummy! That tastes great!
Is there any more broccoli on my plate?"

I'm Gonna Eat Your _____

This game trades on a child's natural possessiveness, and although it doesn't help encourage sharing, it may get them to eat defensively.

1. Tell your child that you're going to eat one of their items (pick a protein or veggie—something they normally don't go for).

2. Move your fork slowly and deliberately toward their plate.

3. If your child is a typical, possessive kid, they'll say something like, "No! That's mine!" Then they'll quickly grab it and shove it in their mouth.

4. Give your child an appropriately silly, disappointed look or an exaggerated look of surprise to guarantee a laugh.

Variation: Tell your child that you want them to feed you an item, and open your mouth wide. Tell them that there's no tricking allowed, and that they definitely can't pretend to give you the item and then place it in their own mouth. Any kid worth their salt will do exactly what you told them not to do, and presto! Another bite—hopefully several—will be taken!

IF THEY'RE ON TO YOU

Just relax. Don't turn meals into a battle—the kid won't starve.

GET YOUR KID TO GO OUT TO DINNER

How can an experience as enjoyable as dining out with your children also be so fear inducing? Will they misbehave? Will they eat anything? Will they fight with their sister or throw the dreaded tantrum? Will the cost of eating out and the added stress make it worth it at all—or should you just get takeout and stay home? Ultimately, it is worth the trouble, because by learning to be open to new experiences, your kids gain a lifelong skill that will serve them (and you) well. But getting there isn't always easy. You need a plan—and that means equipping yourself with some good sneaky tricks.

LAYING THE GROUNDWORK

- Establish a consistent dinnertime routine at home. Make your kid sit at the table, talk in a normal tone, and exhibit good manners—it will pay off.

- If you have a particular restaurant in mind, first try something from its takeout menu, to build familiarity and interest in the food and to get your child used to the flavors or preparation. Then, before you go, review the menu online together. This will speed up the ordering and decision-making and also give you a chance to talk about some of the foods from a comfortable and familiar place: your home.

- On your way to the restaurant, review what is expected from your child before, during, and after the meal—especially if the place has good desserts.

- Try to avoid having a famished child on your hands. A hungry child is an impatient child, and waiting for your meal will be that much harder.

- At the table, try to prevent the endless refilling of water glasses, especially if the drinks come with straws—because, as we all know, things are more fun with straws. A bloated child will not want to eat when the food arrives, but they'll surely be hungry when you get home (probably about two minutes before bedtime).

PRETTY SNEAKY

- Order an appetizer right away so that food arrives quickly, before the main meal. Pick a dish you think your child will like plus a new food or spice they're unfamiliar with. If they like it, great. If not, no problem: it's just an appetizer.

- Wait until after placing your order to go wash your hands together. This will eat (pun intended) into some of the wait time and give your child a chance to explore the restaurant.

- Bring a deck of cards and turn the wait into an opportunity to have fun. Teach your kids a few games at home (doing so in a restaurant is a challenge, what with everything else going on). You can rotate the selection so that everyone gets to play a favorite game.

- If you choose a restaurant serving regional or international food, look up some fun facts about the country or culture and discuss them. Where is the country or area located? How many people live there? Use your phone to point out the location on a map and look up some local landmarks and pastimes.

- Bring paper and markers or crayons and draw while waiting for your meal.

- Help your child order their own meal. (This is where their natural tendency for role-playing and acting will come in handy!)

- Establish a rule that your child must try at least one new food on the table in order to have dessert.

- Take turns picking the restaurant for family events, and start a tradition of letting your child pick the restaurant for their birthday. They will feel more excited and invested in having a good time. (And if one of your kids ruins the experience for another, they lose their next turn to pick.)

- At home, make a game of pretending to eat at a restaurant, with each person playing a different character. Have one child play the parent ordering, paying the bill, or doing something silly. It makes for a good laugh and is something to talk about when dining out. Everyone can observe and learn, so your kids can play more parts in the future.

A LITTLE SNEAKY

"Do you want to go out to _____ or _____?"

"Let's pretend to be somebody else at the restaurant tonight. Who do you want to be?"

I Doubt It! (Dining-Out Edition)

This is a great game for three or more players. Whoever gets rid of all of their cards first wins.

Deal all the cards in the deck to the players. The person who was dealt the ace of clubs starts the game. That player must throw in their ace(s), facedown, while saying how many cards they are putting down. The next person throws in 2s and the next person 3s, always facedown, and so on, following the order in which the cards were dealt.

The thrower must be truthful about the number of cards they put on the table, but they can attempt to fool the other players by putting down cards that aren't the value they're claiming. For example, they may be holding only one 2, but when it is their turn to put down 2s, they can put down a 2 and a 3 facedown and say, "Two 2s."

Once a thrower has made their claim, any other player can say, "I doubt it," until the next player throws. Upon calling "I doubt it," play stops and the cards are turned over to check the thrower's claim. If it was a bluff, the thrower must take the entire pile of cards. If it was not a bluff, the challenger takes the pile. If no one doubts the claim, play continues in the order of the deal.

Feel free to add a "dining-out" component to this game: When a cheater is caught, for example, they have to feed the person of the doubter's choosing a bite of food, in addition to taking the pile!

IF THEY'RE ON TO YOU

Eating dessert first always works!

GET YOUR KID TO TAKE A BATH

Cleanliness is next to godliness, the saying goes. But clearly there were many children who were not briefed on this fact. Some may hate the feel of the bath. Still others may be reluctant to have water splashed on their face or have their toes scrubbed. And some may just find that bath time is a good time to test their independence. Whatever the case, a child must be washed on a fairly regular basis, come hell or belly-button-high water.

LAYING THE GROUNDWORK

- Make sure the water isn't too hot—better a bath that's too cool than one that scalds. Let your child test it first.

- Teach your child how to turn the faucet on and off (stress that this should only be done with a parent in the room), and let them run their own bath. Everyone likes to feel empowered.

- Purchase a vast array of bath toys, ideally with your child's participation. Friendly looking towels and washcloths; plastic ducks, boats, and fish; and bathtub paints and crayons are always winners.

PRETTY SNEAKY

- Mix up bath time for variety: 11:00 A.M. on a rainy Saturday, 4:00 P.M. on a snowy Thursday, or 2:00 P.M. on a hot Sunday—heck, why not take a bath right now? It is "wacky" to do something off schedule in the eyes of a child; it borders on illicit, and thus might make it more enjoyable. Play up the fact that there are no other kids bathing at this time.

- Don't call it bathing—call it swimming. Run the bath extra deep. Offer goggles and water wings to willing participants. Teach your child to blow bubbles, practice the doggie paddle, and float on their back. Research shows that the bath is an excellent way to get infants acclimated to water, increasing the likelihood that they will swim when older. New babies can float on their backs and practice frog kicks, with your support.

- Bathe a bath time toy, with your child's assistance. Have your child get the [DOLL/ANIMAL] ready for the bath and have a towel (a washcloth perhaps) and pajamas ready for after drying off. Ask your child to make sure that the water temperature is OK for the toy, wash the toy, and teach the toy how not to be afraid of the water.

- Mix it up with an occasional bubble bath (for kids older than 3), or take a bottle of blowing bubbles into the tub.

A LITTLE SNEAKY

"Do you want to take a bath or a shower?"
"Do you want to wash your body, or do you want me to wash your body?"
"Do you want to use the purple washcloth or the one shaped like a ladybug?"
"Do you want a bubble bath or a swimming bath tonight?"

THE EENSY-WEENSY SPIDER

There are many songs throughout history related to the joys of bathing. Flex your vocal cords and let out your best rendition of "Splish Splash," "Rubber Duckie," or "Bathtime" (by Raffi). Or just try the bath time version of this classic, soap in hand as you do the motions:

The eensy-weensy spider
Went up your leg today
Down came the water to rinse the dirt away

Out came the soap to scrub a dub with glee
The eensy weensy spider said, "Now you must wash me!"

Replace with other body parts as needed.

Bath Soup

Encourage your child to make you soup in the bath. Allow them to explore your kitchen and pick a set amount of cooking items (three to five) to bring into the bath with them. Wooden spoons, bowls, a whisk, and plastic measuring cups all make wonderful bath toys and allow your budding chef to make endless soups and soufflés in the bath.

Variation: Have your "wizard" or "witch" make you a potion or a spell in the tub. Let them lightly sprinkle it on you, and ask them what they're turning you into. Become the object they specify.

Get into the bath with your child—fully clothed. The sheer absurdity of the situation should make them laugh, and they should be willing to get in themself.

GET YOUR KID TO WASH THEIR HAIR

There comes a time in every child's life (at least a couple of times a week) when the hair simply must be cleaned. For those that prefer the greaseball look, some trickery may be necessary.

LAYING THE GROUNDWORK

- Visit your local drugstore to get your child excited about picking out their first hair product. Let them smell the options, and then pick one. (Make sure it's a children's shampoo and thus "tear free.")

- Give the clean hair lots of press. Make sure you mention how good it smells and how good it feels.

- Teach your child how to tip their head back to avoid getting water in their eyes. Showing what happens first to a doll who doesn't tip its head back can help get the message across.

- Let your child choose, as much as possible, how the hair washing will happen: "Do you want to use this shampoo or that one?" "Do you want to use a cup or a bowl to rinse the soap out?" "Do you want to wash your hair quickly or slowly?"

- Let your child do it themself—with your assistance, of course. Give them a small amount of shampoo, teach them to rub it in and work up a lather, and help them rinse the soap out themself.

PRETTY SNEAKY

- Don't say it's time to wash hair; say it's "time to go to the spa." Treat your child like an adult customer. Ask them for their appointment time and show them the way to the tub. Adopt a silly voice and keep them giggling throughout the experience.

- Who doesn't love a scalp massage? Even the littlest humans can appreciate this luxury. Use this perk to make hair washing a positive experience.

- Teach your child to hold a washcloth tightly over their face (hands at their temples) to keep the water out of their eyes.

- Make a shampoo sculpture. Keep a mirror on hand to show your child what they look like with shampoo on their head. Shape it into a point, a Mohawk, horns, or whatever else comes to mind. Then let them try.

- Run the "Hairy 500"—basically, the "Let's See How Fast We Can Wash Our Hair" game. Competition overcomes kids' reluctance, and before you know it their hair is clean. Count out loud, and write down their time so that they can try to "beat the clock" next time.

"Do you want to wash your hair, or do you want me to?"

"Do you want to put a washcloth over your face or just close your eyes when I rinse your hair?"

"Do you want me to wet your hair with the cup or the faucet tonight?"

I'M GONNA WASH THAT YUCK RIGHT OUT OF MY HAIR

To the tune of "I'm Gonna Wash That Man Right Out of My Hair." Sing this song while washing hair, letting your child suggest the things you need to wash out of their hair (those ladybugs, that dirt, those puppies, etc.).

I'm gonna wash that yuck right out of my hair
I'm gonna wash that yuck right out of my hair
I'm gonna wash that yuck right out of my hair
And leave my dirt behind
I'm gonna wash that _____ right out of my hair

And so on . . .

The One-Armed Wash

Both you and your child pretend that one arm is stuck or glued to your sides—as a result, you have to help each other with the hair-washing process. You squeeze the shampoo into their hand, and they put it in their hair. You both rub it in. They turn on the faucet, you fill the cup and pour while they cover their eyes or tip their head back to rinse.

The Waterfall Game

Pretend that you have found a hidden jungle with an enormous waterfall. You fill big bowls of water and let the water cascade into the bath like a waterfall. Your child can go under the waterfall to rinse their hair. Engage the child in describing the waterfall as well as the pool, the trees, the birds, and the animals that will be using the waterfall to bathe.

IF THEY'RE ON TO YOU

Sometimes kids are actually scared of getting all soaped up. Figure out if your child is afraid or if they just don't want to have their hair washed. If they are afraid, find out more. Is it the shampoo-in-the-eyes concern? Assure them that the shampoo they picked does not sting (and be sure it doesn't). Whatever the concern, get to the root of it and make it go away.

GET YOUR KID TO GO TO BED

"Goodnight, honey," you call, as your wee one walks to their bedroom, puts on their pajamas, crawls under the covers, and puts themselves to bed. Ah, if only this were the case. Maybe it will be, you think, when your kid is a teenager. Until then, you'll have to help them get there every night.

LAYING THE GROUNDWORK

- It's all about the routine. This doesn't necessarily mean you have to be home at the same time every night or even sleep in the same bed every night—but it does mean that wherever you are, whenever it is, the same routine happens (for example, put on pajamas, brush teeth, go to the bathroom, read a story, go to bed). Imagine the bedtime ritual as a train. Your children know that when they get on the train, there is no turning back. Your job is to set up the train and get it out of the station.

- Draw your line in the sand early in the night, and stick to it. If you tell them exactly how many books they can read, count out the books and be sure that they've set aside the right number. If you tell them that you're not coming back in to say goodnight again or sing another song, don't go back, no matter how much they may yell.

- Stay one step ahead of your child at all times. Children are brilliant when it comes to thinking of reasons why they can't go to bed. Preempt their roadblocks. Have water next to the bed. Close the closet door. Put on a night-light. Make sure their teddy bear makes it under the covers.

PRETTY SNEAKY

- Let your child pick which pajamas they wear, and teach them how to put PJs on themselves (even part of the way). This should make your child somewhat less resistant to the process.
- Let them pick which blanket or pillow to use.
- Establish a repertoire of creative methods for getting your child physically into the bed: "Through the cave" (in through the side of the bed and under the covers), "over the clouds" (flying in and landing on the pillow), or "jumping to the moon" (pretending to jump in, with your help) can make the process more fun.
- If your child is sleeping in a bed and not a crib, read and sing to them while lying down next to them rather than sitting up with them in your lap. Often, just getting horizontal makes them realize how tired they are.
- After reading, convince your child to close their eyes as you sing to them or tuck them in—even this simple move can show them how tired they are.
- Have your child put a favorite doll or stuffed animal to bed as part of their pre-bed routine.

A LITTLE SNEAKY

"Do you want to put on your pajamas first or brush your teeth first?"

"Do you want to read two long books or three short books tonight?"

"Do you want to sing the lullaby with me, or should I sing it by myself tonight?"

"Do you want to read books or tell stories?"

GOODNIGHT, MY BEAN

To the tune of "Goodnight Irene."

Monkeys sleep in the treetops
Birds sleep in their nest
[CHILD'S NAME] sleeps in [HIS/HER/THEIR] bed at night
And at naptime when [HE/SHE/THEY] need[s] a rest

My bean, goodni-i-ight
My bean, goodnight
Goodnight my bean
Goodnight my bean
I'll see you in my dreams
Fish sleep in the ocean
Pigs sleep in their pen
Birds sleep in their cages
Although they wake up now and then

My bean, goodni-i-ight
My bean, goodnight
Goodnight my bean
Goodnight my bean
I'll see you in my dreams

GAMES PARENTS PLAY

Let's Tell a Story

Obviously, you don't want to get your kid too worked up at bedtime, so actively engaging them mentally or physically at this time of day isn't really recommended unless you have a desire to fight them to sleep. However, getting them to participate in storytelling with you can be quite enjoyable and relaxing.

Don't put too much pressure on them—make up the story "Mad Libs" style, leaving a blank word every sentence or so to let them feel as if they're directing it. If they really get the hang of it, let them direct the story even further. Here's how to start:

Once upon a time, there was a _____ named _____. This _____ wasn't your average _____. They were very, very _____ because they wanted _____.

And so on . . .

IF THEY'RE ON TO YOU

Sometimes, you just have to say goodnight, shut the door, and go to bed!

GET YOUR KID TO GO TO SLEEP

Sometimes, putting children to bed is the easy part—it's getting them to sleep that's hard. We all have nights when we just can't shut down our brains, and kids do, too. Those are the nights they're in and out of their rooms after you've put them to bed. Maybe there's a big, exciting event taking place the next day, or maybe they're worried about something at school. Whatever it is that's keeping them up, your task is to con your kid into forgetting about it and hitting the hay, so you can, too.

LAYING THE GROUNDWORK

- If there's a clock in your child's room, make sure it doesn't emit light at all times. Often, knowing how late it is causes more stress.

- Before leaving the room after your bedtime routine, ask if there's anything on your child's mind. Talking about problems or anxieties may head off a visit from your child five minutes after you've left the room.

- Teach your child deep-breathing techniques as a means to relax their mind and body. As you read a story or sing a goodnight song, encourage them to inhale to a count of three and exhale to a count of six. Such concentrated breathing will help them focus on the quietness of the moment and the end of the day.

- Give your child a notebook to keep on their nightstand and encourage them to write in it before bed about anything they want. Five minutes of journaling before falling asleep can help children unload things weighing on their minds.

PRETTY SNEAKY

- Institute a short "Do What You Want Session." Let your child do their favorite activity for fifteen minutes—read, write, draw, do yoga, whatever— as long as, for the next fifteen minutes after that, they try to go to sleep. If that doesn't work, let them try it again. Usually, one session is all it takes.

- If your child is anxious and cannot "turn off their brain," tell them to make a "worry list," writing down all the things they're worried about; they can also tell you about the worries if they want. This is a great way to learn about your child's fears and anxieties and provides an opportunity to help them work through major stressors. Have them put the list under their pillow or in a special bag to make the worries go away.

- Tell your child that stories are magical and instruct them to create their own "Story in Your Head." Have them put their head under the covers (or a pillow), close their eyes, and, while breathing in to the count of three and out to the count of six, try to remember every part of their favorite movie or storybook. Often, just closing their eyes and focusing on one thing will help them fall asleep.

- Warm milk with nutmeg does wonders, too.

A LITTLE SNEAKY

"Don't be anxious—sleep will find you. Do you want to read by yourself or write in your journal?"

"Why don't you tell your stuffed animal all the things you're thinking about, then let it cuddle you to sleep?"

"Breathe in and out while you sing a song to yourself in your head."

IF THEY'RE ON TO YOU

Just tell your child not to worry and to read or listen to music until they feel tired. Sometimes you just have to let things work themselves out.

APPENDIX

APPENDIX

The pages that follow offer some useful examples of charts and certificates you might want to use when conning your child. You can feel free to photocopy these pages and utilize the charts as printed (enlarge them to 200 percent when you do). However, if you have time, create the chart from scratch with your child; this will further invest them in the process. Each week, note the things that your child did without prompting or coercion, and give out an award (like a sticker) when a certain number is reached.

_____'S GETTING READY FOR BED CHART

	MONDAY	TUESDAY	WEDNESDAY	THURSDAY	FRIDAY	SATURDAY	SUNDAY
Pajamas							
Brush Teeth							
Floss							
Wash Hands							
Wash Face							
Read Books							

_____'S MAGIC WORDS CHART

	MONDAY	TUESDAY	WEDNESDAY	THURSDAY	FRIDAY	SATURDAY	SUNDAY
Thank You							
Please							
Excuse Me							
May I Be Excused							
I Am Sorry							

_____'S CHORE CHART

	TO BE DONE BY:	STICKER WHEN COMPLETED	TO BE DONE BY:	STICKER WHEN COMPLETED	TO BE DONE BY:	STICKER WHEN COMPLETED
Clean Room						
Make Bed						
Pick Up Toys						
Wash Dishes						

CERTIFICATE OF HEROISM

This certificate hereby certifies that

_____

did something really good. Specifically, that

_____

_____

and is officially a
HERO.

ABOUT THE AUTHORS

David Borgenicht is a *New York Times* best-selling author and the creator of the iconic Worst-Case Scenario Survival Handbook series. He is also the founder of Quirk Books and, more importantly, is the father of two clever and now adult children, Sophie and Max. He lives in Pennsylvania.

James Grace is the coauthor of several books, including the *New York Times* best seller *The Worst-Case Scenario Survival Handbook: Golf*. He is a lawyer and runs a nonprofit that supports artists and arts organizations. He lives in Massachusetts with his wife, Lisa, and is the father of three crafty and now adult kids, Avery, Cooper, and Dustin.

ACKNOWLEDGMENTS

David Borgenicht: If it takes a village to raise a child, then it takes at least a small hamlet or burg to write a book about raising children—and this book is no exception. I'd like thank our original editor, Erin Slonaker, and our reboot editor, Jess Zimmerman, for shepherding this through! And of course, I'd like to thank the many moms and dads who contributed their knowledge of parental grift, including my own parents, Louis and Nancy; my brother, Joe, and his wife, Melanie. Finally, I have to thank Suzanne Simons and my children, Sophie and Max—without whom this book definitely wouldn't have been possible, or necessary.

James Grace: I often feel like I am in the movie *The Sting*, constantly orchestrating one long con. The supporting cast in my movie is the great friends and family that I have learned from and that have helped me tap into my best sneakiness. I want to thank them for all of their support, shared techniques, and time. The casting of my wife, Lisa Goldblatt Grace, was the key to everything. She helped craft this book, and without her this whole parenting thing would be a lot less fun. Robin Alperin deserves great credit for all her work on the book. Robin has worked with kids for many years as a preschool teacher and mom, and her advice and research were invaluable. Other people that shared their sneakiness include Kathy Reed, Dr. Anthony Compagnone, Krista Harte Sasaman, and the king and queen of it all: Mama and Papa Grace.